Stow Your Luggage When Dating

Advance Praise for *Stow Your Luggage When Dating*

Marlisse takes great care to focus on prioritizing self-worth instead of pushing for a dating "win." This important shift will help readers start an authentic search in this increasingly complicated modern dating world.

> **-Hallie Beaune,** co-author, *The Naked Pint: An Unadulterated Guide To Craft Beer*

You really need to call her Dr. Love because Marlisse is one of the smartest psychotherapists/dating coaches I know. If you're single and ready to have a healthy relationship now, Marlisse's book will help guide you quickly and easily through the dating process without a bunch of complex ideas or fluff. She'll just hold your hand and give you simple tips, suggestions, and guidance on dating and how to find your right partner. This is definite must read!

> **-Preston Rahn,** #1 best-selling author, entrepreneur, consultant

Stow Your Luggage When Dating is for anyone ready to approach love in a smart, healthy way. Unpack what you're carrying and explore an authentic journey into the world of dating today. Marlisse delivers a fresh, exciting roadmap to navigating the pool. Ready to jump in?

> **-Andrea Stephens,** N.E.L.L. (Not Exactly Lazy Leisure)

Stow Your Luggage When Dating is a fascinating and enormously useful guide to one of life's most important ventures-finding and sustaining a secure, satisfying loving relationship. The author Marlisse Testa uses her experience as a psychotherapist, and offers powerful tips to improve your self-esteem, strengthen your confidence and find the relationship you've always dreamed of! The book is enriched with interesting and well-designed exercises, which are effective to attract a long-lasting love. It provides deep insights and invaluable skills that will benefit every reader! As a professional matchmaker of twelve years, I highly recommend reading this book as it should be the "go to" book for all singles!!

-Cheryl Maida, matchmaker

As a single, working professional, the work-life balance is often a struggle. Marlisse's book, *Stow Your Luggage When Dating,* has been essential in helping me quickly navigate the dating scene to create a true partnership while maintaining personal boundaries. I recommend this book as a guide for anyone searching to heal from relational trauma.

-Dr. Stephanie Renfrow, clinical neuropsychologist

I met Marlisse Testa in 2015. Marlisse has helped me not only find my self-worth and authentic self, but also helped me believe and have complete confidence in myself! *Stow Your Luggage When Dating* will help so many individuals who get stuck within their own selves and truly find the courage to get back out there. I was that person, and with Marlisse's help and her strategies, she really helped me to find my self-worth and, for the first time, have complete confidence in myself. And for that, I am eternally grateful to have Marlisse in my life!

-Jason M. Trexler, member of the service industry

If you've ever asked yourself, "Why isn't there a manual to tell me the best way to date?!" then this book is for you! Written by a licensed mental health professional with over twenty years of experience working with individuals and couples on how to build and maintain healthy relationships, this book will guide you through the many challenges and questions of "DATING." *Stow Your Luggage When Dating* is written with a confident and an easy-to-follow format, along with several helpful worksheets and exercises that walk you through important aspects to consider when deciding on who and how to date.

-Anastasia Leondis, LMHC, NCC, QS

As a leadership coach that awakens people to see their highest potential as their authentic selves—I always point out the profound impact that your marriage or life partner has on maintaining or becoming WHOLE in who they are because that is what makes the healthiest relationships. Yet in today's social and digital culture, defining and finding the right partner has become so complex. Singles need a dating coach and therapist to help them define a new way of understanding themselves, who they seek, and how they seek them in the context of dating, and Marlisse Testa's critical book is that guide.

-Claudia Chan, author of *This Is How We Rise*, founder of S.H.E. Summit, creator of The Whole-Life Leadership Framework

STOW YOUR LUGGAGE WHEN DATING

Practical Ways to Get
Back into Dating
While Putting Your
Past Behind You
to Have a Healthy,
Vibrant, and
Lasting Relationship

MARLISSE TESTA, LMHC

NEW YORK

LONDON • NASHVILLE • MELBOURNE • VANCOUVER

Stow Your Luggage When Dating

Practical Ways to Get Back into Dating While Putting Your Past Behind You to Have a Healthy, Vibrant, and Lasting Relationship

Published in New York, New York, by Morgan James Publishing. Morgan James is a trademark of Morgan James, LLC. www.MorganJamesPublishing.com

Proudly distributed by Ingram Publisher Services.

Morgan James BOGO™

A **FREE** ebook edition is available for you or a friend with the purchase of this print book.

CLEARLY SIGN YOUR NAME ABOVE

Instructions to claim your free ebook edition:
1. Visit MorganJamesBOGO.com
2. Sign your name CLEARLY in the space above
3. Complete the form and submit a photo of this entire page
4. You or your friend can download the ebook to your preferred device

ISBN 9781631959011 paperback
ISBN 9781631959028 ebook
Library of Congress Control Number:
2022932539

Cover & Interior Design by:
Christopher Kirk
www.GFSstudio.com

Morgan James PUBLISHING

Builds

with...

Habitat for Humanity®
Peninsula and
Greater Williamsburg

Morgan James is a proud partner of Habitat for Humanity Peninsula and Greater Williamsburg. Partners in building since 2006.

Get involved today! Visit MorganJamesPublishing.com/giving-back

This book is dedicated to all the single people out there,
looking for some type of clarity or support.
I got your back!

Table of Contents

Acknowledgments

The time, creativity, knowledge, and foresight that went into this book took about ten years of writing, thinking, and honing. Its information comes from personal experience and feedback from others I have guided through their dating journey. This book is practical and filled with valuable skills. It is meant to help mold you into a more efficient dater that fits your lifestyle.

My goal is to create a platform where people don't stay in unhealthy relationships and help people heal from their past so they don't miss out on healthy relationships.

We learned many things through our upbringing and in our school institutions, but I bet most of us didn't learn healthy relationship skills, which may be the most essential tools to have in life. Relationships are inherent. We have them in all areas, all levels, and in all venues. We must master the ability to make and maintain relationships, which brings us to the ability to select a healthy partner.

I want to thank all the individuals that have encouraged me along the way. All of my friends were invaluable in writing this book, but especially my dear friend, Diana, whom I supported and guided after her divorce, faithfully using these exact ingredients to get her back on her feet to find a healthy relationship. This fabulous woman motivated me to finish writing this book to help others— just as I assisted her, and now, she is currently happy and engaged!

After writing, my amazing parents, Carol and Mike, supported me in helping find the people to make this book come to life. My loving mother, who assisted in my first edit, and my helpful father for his legal advice, all of the work happening between our busy schedules. Also, my dear friend Joe, who assisted me with endless legal advice.

I want to thank the Morgan James Publishing team, especially David Hancock, for selecting me and my work. To all of the staff for the effort, phone calls, and time devoted to creating this modern-age dating book. My editors, Susanne Hale and Cortney Donelson, for editing and formatting all the details. These key people are the backbone of this success.

I also want to thank my incredibly insightful daughter, Lexi, who listens and supports me more than she is aware. I hear her guiding her friends. Life would not be as wonderful or complete without her.

May you all find what you're seeking, and I hope this book becomes a compass, aiding you to find it.

Foreword

I want to share how I met the amazing Marlisse Testa and why you should read her incredible book about dating. I met Marlisse while doing my internship, and she became more than a mentor to me. She is the epitome of strength, resilience, and charisma. In *Stow Your Luggage When Dating*, you will feel her encouraging support, serving as a cheerleader for you along the dating journey, just like she does for me and so many others. The strategies she taught me, which I continue to use in my sessions with clients and for myself, are now in print—a resource to help everybody.

Dating can be complicated, and *Stow Your Luggage When Dating* gives you the tools to master it. If you are single and dating, out of a marriage or a relationship, or want to help others in the dating field, this book is one thousand percent for you! Put all of the other dating books down! This book is fun, to the point, and witty. Marlisse has been in the coaching and counseling field for over twenty years and has personal and professional dating experience. She is the go-to person for answering questions on and about dating. She has found success in helping clients meet their healthy, vibrant, everlasting mates.

The reason this book was so powerful for me is that it hits the nail on the head of why so many people are single today or choosing relationships that fail. The keyword here is *choosing* since singleness and engaging with poor matches *are* choices. Selecting the right partner becomes more effortless with this book. No one taught us how to heal and evolve from past relationships, including our parents who may have stayed together forever. This book will teach you how to get ready for a healthy relationship and how to find an equivalent partner who is ready too.

It's a "throw in your pocket" kind of book, and you can take it out when needed, over and over again, until you meet your person. It will guide you in becoming more self-aware of where and what your needs are right now.

I continue to work with Marlisse in many ways. We attend training together, and we aim to keep our treatment plans relevant to the modern, evolving world. This book provides exactly that: modern strategies for dating in today's world. Because we all know dating isn't always easy. But Marlisse will change your perspective!

Read the book, do the worksheets, and benefit from those changes!

-**Terri Samuels,** licensed mental health counselor
and nationally certified counselor

Introduction

The Basics

I f you are one of the millions of people out there who are single and looking for some clarity, I hope to give it to you today! The dating world is rapidly changing, and I am sure meeting people now is very different from the last time you were out there single and dating. Yes, it is confusing and exciting all at the same time. Welcome to the new dating world.

I'm not here to be your genie or your wing woman, but I can give you some tips and guidance to help you navigate the new dating jungle.

First, you need to be self-aware so you can figure out where you are and what your needs are at this time.

Second, you need to heal from your past and learn new methods for finding healthy relationships.

And **third**, you should have a good sense of who you are (self-worth) and what is important to you as far as friends, family, and hobbies and determine how you will use your new skills.

Stow Your Luggage When Dating is for anyone single and ready to get back out there and find a healthy partner. This is not a rule book or a black book. Each chapter will give you suggestions to use when dating and will explain why you may want to use them. You will make your decisions based on this information and what fits your life.

You may be recently divorced, separated, or just out of a short-term or long-term relationship. Maybe you took a year to soul search, and now, you are ready to "get back on the horse." Maybe you have blocked out all emotions and feel numb or perhaps you threw yourself into your career. Now, you may be wanting more from and for your life. The question is: what do you want for your life at this moment? To date, to hook up, to have a causal relationship, or do you want something more serious?

This can be a tricky question. Even if you are ready for a serious relationship, you must reset your mindset. When dating, the long-term goal may be to find that *one* person, the one you want to spend your life with, but you won't know who that person is until you find them. In the meantime, stay open to dating and riding the wave while you figure it out. Quite frankly, that's the most honest you can be—to yourself and others. For those individuals who want to develop something faster or who want a finite response, I don't believe it is possible at the very beginning.

Not only am I a psychotherapist with twenty years of experience assisting thousands of individuals like yourself in dating, but I am also an avid dater myself. I am on the same journey and use these techniques I'm going to share in the following chapters. The reason I emphasize healing from the past before moving forward in a new relationship is, without healing, many people get stuck. This is exactly what happened to me and many of my clients. Skipping the healing step led me to date the wrong people over and over again.

Know this: patterns can be changed with therapy. I took pleasure—and still do—in watching my clients and friends heal from their past, get back out there, and meet healthy people to share their lives with. I've seen it happen nearly every day.

Dating and finding a relationship take time. Without dating, and making healthy choices as you do, you are only setting yourself up for unhappiness. Remember, love is a choice, and selection is extremely important. I'm here to help you wisely choose the person you want to share your life with. Do not let them choose you.

The following chapters are all about you and the process of dating and finding your partner. There is no implicit order for reading *Stow Your Luggage When Dating*. I encourage you to jump around and use this book as a tool, not read it as you would a novel. I will explain my ideas and give you precise steps throughout the process. I have also created hands-on worksheets, which you can fill out along the way. If you don't need the steps or don't want to use the resources, skip them. This is your journey. What you put into it will affect what you get out of it.

This book is an excellent way to get started *now*. My desire is that this book makes you say "WOW! I need to work on myself!" Or, I hope it validates the idea that you are in an ideal dating space, and these are precisely the steps you needed to confirm. Of course, you may also use this book while in therapy—or in place of it. Either way, let's get you started!

**Stow Your Luggage When Dating is an opportunity
to create hope, awareness, and skills
for those of you who are ready to date again.**

Part 1

Where are you?
What do you want from a partner?

Get a Grip
And Stay Your Authentic Self!

I want to use this opportunity to remind each of you how amazing and unique you are. Everyone's journey is different; some wind, some twist, some bounce up and down, and some may seem straight. Some people will find epic forever love, while others will discover mini romances throughout their lives. Please don't compare yourself to others, as we are all on our own journeys that may unfold differently throughout our lifetimes.

As humans, we feel rejection and self-doubt, especially when comparing ourselves to others. Stay focused on yourself and what you have learned (and will learn) from each relationship, and keep growing and moving forward to find what you want from a partner. More people are living alone each day, refusing to settle, taking their time finding the right person, and finding the person with the right compatibilities that will allow love to foster and grow.

It's hard, especially when we were never taught how to find a healthy partner, primarily relying on emotions and passion at first sight. Those are great initial indicators, but they don't last without finding a person with the right compatibilities (e.g., religious beliefs, money or status, values, and communication), along with healthy physical attraction, which are the ingredients in a recipe for building love. With love comes butterflies, passion, and emotions that will last much longer as you intentionally maintain them.

Love is a choice.

Life is about living and having a unique story to tell. Try not to compare or settle! The world is full of millions of singles. You have the opportunity to take your pick. On you journey, remember to have fun and be your awesome self!

Enjoy your journey and keep moving.

Dating Tip

There is no rejection in dating.
If you or your date are not connecting, move on.
Be open to finding a mutual connection.

Dating Tip

Eager comes across as too clingy,
whereas *cool* is more confident.

Chapter 1

Ready, Set, Date

Many people are searching for their good fit at age thirty, forty, or fifty years old (and older). Dating in a world where you work, take care of kids and pets, and most likely do a hundred other things that you cannot categorize can be challenging. Each of us has a past that includes relationships or marriages that have left us with open wounds. We walk into new relationships with *all of these wounds*. Finding connections seems to get more challenging and complex while our ability to love gets stronger and stronger.

We may have an idea of what we want from a partner and what we are looking for when re-entering the dating arena. We may even have a list, identifying the traits or relationship characteristics that we want, and we are aware of what we don't like. Dating means we are going out, on the lookout for all of it. Later in this chapter, I will discuss how to create your list of what you want.

You have way more tools than you think you do! As you continue to read, you may be reminded of the tools you already possess and how you can use them.

When dating, we need to use every available arena to meet people, especially in our technologically-advanced era. This means meeting people while out, through friends, on dating sites, through social media, with dating services, and even at the grocery store. There are many more ways to get yourself noticed than in pre-technology times. Therefore, it is a good idea to stay open to all ideas and use them to your advantage.

Now, let's discuss what exactly you are looking for in a partner. First, there is appearance and what you find attractive. This can vary from person to person. You may find that you have a particular attraction or that your desires change. It's all OK.

First, determine what body type you prefer: thin, athletic, chubby, or overweight. What about height? Short, average, or tall? Some people like long and straight hair; some prefer curly, and some would choose bald. Also, what color eyes, hair, and skin type do you find attractive? Start to think about what you like . . . or you may find the physical attributes are not important to you at all.

Second, is the personality of an individual. Do you like outgoing individuals or quiet ones? Introverted or extroverted? Intellectual or street-smart people? Would you prefer a serious-natured person or a funny, silly person? These are great questions you need to ask yourself.

Third, what type of character do you like: hard-working, career-oriented, or someone who likes to fly by the seat of their pants? Do you want stability over excitement and travel? Do you want them to have the same core values? As I take you through this book, I hope you will start to discover more of what interests you.

I want you to become proficient at also seeing what you *don't like* in a partner. This will save you time when dating. The following chapters will discuss many criteria to consider, including kids and parenting styles, commonalities, respect and adjustability, and when to set boundaries. Let's start with a basic list. Grab a pencil with a good eraser.

Create a list of what you want in a partner. Write *ten* characteristics that you want your next partner to possess (examples: good-looking, intelligent, honest, responsible, a provider, healthy). Your completed list will provide you with specifics as to what you are looking for in a partner.

List 10 must-haves in your next partner:

1. _____

2. _____

3. _____

4. _____

5. _____

6. _____

7. _____

8. _____

9. _____

10. _____

Now circle the five of them that seem most important to you.

These five things compile your non-negotiables list. This list will change as you go through the dating process. It can be modified as your transformation continues. It is not set in stone!

Chapter 2

The Ice Cream Theory

I n the ice cream theory, I will be describing each of us as an individual, using the analogy of an ice cream cone. I will explain why it is vital to stay true to yourself. *You* are in charge of your life, and *you* are the only one who can create total **happiness** for yourself. Other people are additions to our lives, but at the end of the day, all we need is **ourselves.** This realization is ultimately the state of mind we should all be seeking.

Imagine a big ice cream store. Now, pick your favorite flavor of ice cream, whether it's vanilla or chocolate, or even rum raisin.

Great! Next, select your cone. Is it a sugar cone or a waffle cone? OK, fantastic! Finally, choose your toppings: sprinkles, hot fudge, or even a few nuts. Ha!

The cone in your ice cream dessert represents your ethics, morals, and beliefs. They include your religion, your sense of right from wrong, the solid core of who you are, and your moral compass. These are the qualities about you that never really change so that when you encounter friends years later, it often feels as if you saw them yesterday because you are who you are at your core, and that never changes.

Now, let's talk about your ice cream! Your ice cream is all the things you like and appreciate. These are your hobbies, the clothes you wear, what social media you engage with, and the career you choose. It is all the things that satisfy you and make you happy. Perhaps your ice cream is exercise or tennis, a Friday night movie night with your friends, or cuddling up with your dog or cat on a cold night. Your ice cream may consist of such things as your preferred music, favorite books, or even your favorite pillow. These are the things about you that you *enjoy* but may have varying aspects and can change, such as your favorite, food, color, or music. If we stop doing the things we love or others stop us from doing the things that make us happy, our ice cream may begin to melt. We are the only ones who can keep our ice cream intact. To avoid melting, we must stay in tune with ourselves, our self-care, and our needs.

The toppings on our ice cream cone represent the additions to your life: the sprinkles, nuts, whipped cream, or maybe some chocolate syrup. They are the people you choose to add to your world. I want to remind you that *you* pick and choose who *you* want to share your life with. For this reason, you can **be picky**. Only let the people who are good to you and for you into that special place. I always tell people that it is better to be alone than to keep bad company. The toppings to your ice cream are your friends, co-workers, lovers, and even your family members.

There are many types of people out there. Throughout life, we will most likely experience them all. Some people are selfish, lost, toxic, addicts, hurt, and maybe even co-dependent individuals, who will try to eat your ice cream and attempt to crack your cone. When you are vulnerable or naïve, this can happen quickly, but as you learn to be more mindful, you will choose healthier friends. There are, unfortunately, sneaky people who will behave maliciously or manipulatively. They know what they are doing and will eat your ice cream and crack your cone to fulfill their own needs. I will discuss these individuals in detail in the "Be Mindful" section of this book. Everyone must get better at reading others and themselves. Your body will tell you when people are not suitable for you by giving you a gut, anxious, or even sick feeling, but you must listen.

Your number one job is to stay focused on yourself and your inner voice. You can have the ability to be happy—and stay happy—by doing the things that create inner happiness. (Happiness is a relative term, so let's not get carried away either.) Be aware of who you let into your life and take your time trusting and getting close. If this is going to be a lifelong friend or a long-term romantic relationship, you have all the time in the world to get to know each other. Be patient.

**Bad-intentioned people will fade away
if you take the time to see them for who they are.**

Fill Out Your Ice Cream Cone Theory

People you chose to share your life with

Things that make you happy

Your core values

Chapter 3

Know Your Worth

We all want to feel loved, liked, admired, and attractive. We witness this need played out in life, the movies, and on social media, and we hear it in our music lyrics. Being wanted and feeling attractive is a huge part of our feelings of belonging. When we find our authentic selves, I'm here to tell you that need for attention and attraction decreases as we develop a good sense of family, friends, and a career or hobby that defines who we are. This superficial thinking is a social perception, and it's not real. While not comparing yourself with others, discovering yourself first and foremost are both topics I capture in this book. It would be best if you found your own beautiful or handsome self before you can get back into dating.

Dating will lead to self-doubt and have you questioning your self-worth and what you want from a mate from time to time, and you must have a solid sense of self and what you want to get through dating. No one can make you feel good about yourself but you. Yes, you have your support system and yes, they are there and helpful, but the job is ultimately yours. We date to find love and companionship, not to find someone to make us feel better about ourselves. It would be unfair to give that job to anyone else.

When dating, there are things you should stay clear of if you want to be successful. One must accept there will be mutual and non-mutual attractions, and most people are poor communicators and won't tell you straight-up how they feel. If your date does not text you or call you back, they are not interested. Your mindset must change in these situations. If someone is not interested in you, this means they are not your person. Why would you push for someone who doesn't feel the same way as you when you can quickly go out and find another who does? I am aware it will take time. It is better to be alone and looking for the right one who brings healthy, vibrant, lasting love than to push someone into feeling something they do not. Some people are going to find you very attractive, and others will not. If they don't appreciate your unique qualities, just wait, and someone else will. Then, it will be their loss, indeed! That's what makes the world go round—there's someone for everyone.

The strongest, bravest people are out there dating—not settling—and looking for their partners. You are the dating warriors, the individuals who won't get knocked down when someone is not interested or you discover after three dates that they are not emotionally available. Or maybe, after three months, when their core is exposed, you realize you don't like their moral compass. You will brush it off, lick your wounds, and remind yourself what you're looking for because you deserve all of it, and you will get up and back into the dating ring. This process is all part of dating and putting yourself out there. It's the only way to do it. What is life without love? That's the prize we are all seeking: mutual, undying love.

When your date doesn't call, it's OK. When your date said they would call but doesn't, that is fine too. When they cancel and don't recommit, great; these choices show you they are not the one. You don't want any of that. These are all signs that you should walk away. It does not mean calling and texting them, blowing up their phone, and confronting them about their behaviors is the way to go. You know the answer, so why do you need to hear it? Silence is your best friend, and if you need to discuss emotions, talk to a friend to help you process them. Remember, your person will not make you feel bad, and if they do, let it serve as a warning sign that they are likely not the right match. I call this weeding out the undesirables.

You deserve the best; take your time and find it!

Chapter 4

Hold on Loosely

Not everyone has healthy boundaries. These are modeled and taught during domestication and, sometimes, later through other healthy adult relationships or by seeing a therapist. But there are people of all ages who still do not have a good grasp of or are not aware of healthy boundaries.

Healthy boundaries are being able to say no and making yourself a priority. It's an ability to express your feelings and needs clearly to others, be heard, listen to your own feelings, and be self-aware of what and why you are feeling them. Most of all, creating these healthy boundaries is done by respecting other people's space and time and valuing them as you would yourself.

With boundaries you ask permission before using something when it is not yours; it is calling someone before popping over to their house or job. It requires asking if they want your opinion without just presenting it, and it's not expecting anything from anyone unless asked or discussed.

Learning healthy dating boundaries is another great tool for your dating toolbox. It is important to recognize that whomever you are dating also understands healthy boundaries in a healthy relationship of any kind.

Let's talk about what boundaries in dating look like and how to keep your boundaries intact.

First, having boundaries means you're going to do what you say and say what you do. If you are going to call, call! If someone tells you they will call you back, you wait. If someone is busy, ask them to contact you when they are not and wait. If you're going on a date, you're going on a date. If you change your mind, you need to inform the other person and respect their time. Please don't play unhealthy games; it's crucial to be clear and transparent.

Second, there are boundaries as far as personal space and being respectful of entering their space. Learning to read body language and asking questions always helps when you are uncertain about entering someone's space. This pertains to the person you are dating, friends, and the people around you and how they set their boundaries when spending time alone or within a group. For example, being too touchy with the opposite sex—or the same sex, depending on your sexual preference—may not present as a clear boundary. Many people have friends of all genders that are not romantic interests. Friend or not, when you are dating someone, there is a level of respect that everyone should have. This is healthy. One must learn how to handle these types of situations by saying no and expressing how certain things make you feel. (Personal space boundary encroachment is a red flag, so tuck it away in your mental file and watch to see if it happens again.)

Third, when dating people, they may just show up at your home or work; they may start friending all your friends on social media, or maybe they invite themselves out with you and your friends on a Friday night. These are all unhealthy boundaries. When boundaries are unclear, it opens up the door to jealousy, distrust, and suffocation. This person must ask and respect your space, time, and person. This individual may be amazingly good-looking, but their behaviors are unhealthy, and your body should feel it. Please listen and correct it by setting firm healthy boundaries. If the behaviors continue after you set these boundaries, then maybe it is time to say goodbye.

Healthy boundaries are essential to a lasting, vibrant relationship. However, if you find you're not clear on how to set them or if you think your limits are not healthy, please reach out for support. A therapist can assist you in developing and expressing boundaries in a safe environment, free from judgment.

Set healthy boundaries from the start!

Notes

Part
II

The tools to get you started.

Don't Go Shopping When . . .

O nce you discover your needs and desires in life, it is the best time to start shopping. When you feel empty inside or are filling a hole of loneliness or sadness, you will settle for whoever makes you feel better. Using the analogy "never go food shopping when you are hungry," the same premise holds in dating. You should not date when you are horny. When you feel good about yourself and your life, and everything feels complete except for wanting someone to share it with you, it is a good sign that you are ready to start dating and attracting the right kind of person.

When you are hungry and thirsty for someone to make all of your empty feelings go away, you will find the wrong person. When filling your emotional void, you will not find a healthy relationship. Think about being hungry at the market. You may open a bag of chips and eat them while shopping for pre-made, unhealthy, fast foods. When you are not hungry, you are more likely to make healthier choices to fill your shopping cart.

I want to stress the word **self-awareness**, which is hard to learn but essential to master. You must be aware of what you are doing and thinking, and *why*, to create the change you need.

Dating Tip

Stop fantasizing, and stay in the present!
Keep conversations to near-future talk.
Avoid future planning, as this person may not get there.

Dating Tip

When noticing red flags in your dates,
file them away as you determine
which ones are non-negotiable or temporary.
When you start to see an unacceptable pattern of behavior
or a non-negotiable red flag, congratulate yourself for spotting it
because those red-flag issues will slowly increase in frequency.

Chapter 5

Dating Takes Time, Like Fine Wine

Dating takes time! It takes a lot of searching, like looking for the right pair of shoes, a cool set of shades, or the perfect weekend getaway. But when meeting diverse people and starting to feel connections, it is wise to try them on in your life.

Once you have gone on four to eight dates and established a good fit for both of you, it is a good time to open them up and try them on in all of the other areas in your life. It is wise to see if they fit all of your sides: your fun/creative side, your intellectual side, your work/colleague side, your friend/family side, and at a later point, your intimate side. Remember, moving too fast or forcing a round peg into a square hole can ruin a good thing, just as moving too slowly or reading too much into something can make a date fizzle out. Being able to coast in the middle is your best bet as you get to know prospective partners.

Dating more than one person at a time is the most practical and unspoken way to go. It keeps you from jumping into a relationship too quickly, blind to any red flags or the ability to see the person in front of you. When dating two or three potential partners, you keep a level head. You can also compare traits, and assess how they all handle different situations, giving you the space to read without emotion. This way, as you are not yet emotionally invested, it is easier to walk away when a red flag or a non-negotiable arises—in part because you have two other dates on which you can shift your focus.

If you want to date one person at a time because you find multiple dating to be too tricky or it's simply not your style, then proceed slowly and with caution. Try to stay busy, keep your boundaries, and allow the dating process to evolve healthily. This will help you identify the things you want and don't want from this person, and once again, create a window for you to leave if necessary.

As the dating process progresses and you believe one of the suitors has many of the qualities you want and fits most or all of your sides, you may also feel the connection has started to grow deeper. You may want to inform them that you no longer wish to date other people and focus on only them at this time. This is, of course, only viable if they fit your top five non-negotiables and they fit all of the sides of you as a person.

Your date may reply that they feel the same way, placing you both on the same page. However, your date may not feel the same way. At this point, you can continue to see where the dating goes until they are ready to commit to you. Create a timeline, in the meantime, which you are comfortable with that sets parameters for how long you will invest in them while waiting. You can also decide to gracefully walk away, knowing that if they don't feel the same way about only dating each other now, they may never feel this way. This is your decision. When things are right, they keep moving. When things are not right, there is a push and pull. All of this is OK as you figure it out because we don't want to rush or force anything. You may end up with a great friend or great business contact rather than a dating or intimate partner. Just remember, if it is supposed to work out, it will, and if not, then you are saving yourself from future heartache.

There will come a time in your dating process—after three to eight dates, give or take—that you might realize your date is not a compatible match. Some areas may be flowing, but others are not. It is much easier to break things off after three dates than at seven or eight dates as you are two months in and people generally have more emotions at that time.

Here are a few ways to communicate that you are no longer interested, as no one likes to be the bearer of bad news. Calling or meeting up with your date to explain how you feel is ideal since it is always OK to discontinue a dating relationship if it's not what you want. You can send a nice text message stating the time you had was great, but you don't feel there is enough compatibility, and you wish them all the best. I personally like these high roads. But you can space out phone calls and text messages and have them fade away, but they may confront you later. I suggest reversing the roles and doing what you would want someone to do for you. Whatever you decide, you need to get comfortable with it because ending things with the wrong people enables you to find the right person.

It can take lots of dates before you find a solid connection with someone. As the saying goes, one must kiss a lot of toads before they find their prince or princess. Dating is about being open to meeting someone and possibly falling in love. Remember: what you see is what you get. You are not there to change people, so if you don't like what you see about your date, then it is time to walk away.

How will you assess your dates?

Look for red flags: things you don't want in a partner or characteristics that can lead to things you don't want from a partner, such as a quick temper, excessive drinking, or a shallow character.

Look for compatibilities and commonalities. For instance, you both like to go to the beach, you both love having dinner parties, or both enjoy reading as a great pastime.

Listen to them speak about past relationships, parental relationships, and who they spend time with now. Are they talking poorly about people? Do they learn from relationships?

What are their passions? Knowing this will identify if they are living a fulfilling life.

Chapter 6

Don't Forget to Wear Your Armor

Do not leave the house without putting on your **armor.** I mean it! This is just a date; check your emotions at the door. This is a casual, fun time out with a new person. Emotions should not come into play in the beginning. Yes, I know what some of you are thinking: "I wear my emotions on my sleeve." My response is, for now, cover your sleeve with armor. This could save you from unnecessary heartache. To be honest, your heart does not choose your partner, your head does. Then your head gives your heart permission to follow. If our emotions were to run our lives, we would be in serious trouble. So why do we do it in our love lives?

Emotions are extreme and powerful, which is why it is crucial to learn how to understand and control them. Emotions can be strong and influence you to make poor decisions that conflict with what you know to be right and true. Think about your first love, the very first time you had strong feelings. If your parents did not like your partner, you would run away or do anything to rail against all good judgment.

This is not meant to imply emotions are bad. Love is an amazing and wonderful emotion. We all want love, but please keep your emotions in check, especially when you first meet someone. There is no need to rush and waste a fantastic experience on the wrong person. Trust me!

There is a difference between being authentic and open with a person you are dating and feeling emotional about a person you are dating, which can lead to fantasizing.

Fantasizing about a future with someone you just met can only create false expectations and the inability to gradually get to know your date authentically and organically. On each date, stay in the present and enjoy the quality of time you spend with one another. Try not to look too far into the future. This can cause one person to get further along in the relationship than the other, which makes it difficult to remain in the reality. You are just dating. So keep it real.

Some of you may want to rush into a relationship because that may be all you know after a long-term relationship or marriage. However, especially after divorce, we tend to go back to our dating experience and try to reenact what we did the first time. This is known as "staying in dating patterns," which may be an area you could work on with a therapist. I will discuss this further in a future chapter. Also, understand that this generation is very different; as times change, dating changes too.

Here are three tips to keep your emotions in check when dating:

First, do not overthink the date. This individual may end up a potential love interest, a friend, or someone you may never see again.

Second, remember less is more. Brief texting and talking between dates are ideal. If you are both interested in one another, another date will be set to continue getting to get to know each other. Try to leave *space for the chase!*

Third, before, during, and after the date, keep your thoughts lighthearted, have fun, and then go back to you and *your* life. Each date should increasingly improve after the first, and that first shouldn't be a mind-blowing experience, which might raise a huge red flag.

Do not leave the house without putting on your ARMOR!

Chapter 7

If You Don't Play, You Can't Win

You can tell me and the world all you want that you do not play games and you do not want a person who does. The problem is, you will be single for a while or end up in a series of short-term relationships until you grasp this concept: We all play games at the beginning.

People are like opposite sides of magnets when dating, and when someone tries to get too close, the other person will pull away. We should not want a clingy or needy partner in our lives unless we are co-dependent. Before you begin dating, it is a good time to evaluate and possibly reconstruct your "cling status."

Playing games is a fantastic way to weed out the undesirables and keep the worthy candidates around. It takes time to interpret the players and determine their genuine motives and goals. That is why, in the beginning, dating means meeting and going out with more than one person at a time. *This allows you to evaluate who should remain in the game and who falls off.* In the end, you will have one awesome date still standing, or you will get three more dates and start again.

There is a difference between playing games because you want a relationship and playing games to get short-term pleasure. There are people out there who will tell you precisely what you want to hear to get what they want, such as sex, and never call you again. Avoiding these pitfalls is why playing healthy games is important to determine who wants what from the beginning while learning to *read between the lies and the lines.*

Dating without games would be the part of the process where two people share they are ready for commitment and discuss the relationship's details. When done prematurely, this is a total turn-off, as you are both *strangers* to one another. When these sorts of things are done hastily, the recipe for love becomes spoiled. Also referred to as giving all your cookies away, this is not advisable in the early stages. A healthy mystery is a vital ingredient to a good start.

When looking to be in a healthy relationship, keep communication open and be honest. State what you are looking for while having fun and meeting new people, which can be exciting when you create a connection or find commonalities. Try to create space between the dates and communication. Use the ping-pong analogy when texting (wait for a reply before texting again) and try not to be too coy. Try to be fun, perhaps by sending pictures instead of words to say hello. Make communications clear and upbeat. Try not to always be available and suggest alternatives of when you are available.

We all want to be in a healthy relationship. When using these simple games, you will start to create a connection or quickly find out if you're not compatible. The term *games,* when concerning dating, is used negatively in our society. As children, we loved games. However, when referring to dating games, changing your mindset is crucial. Playing games with your partner carries over to successful long-term relationships and marriages. Don't discount the pleasure and the fun banter between healthy adults, as it is part of the enjoyment.

Stay true to yourself and let the games begin.

Tips on Healthy Games:

When playing ping-pong with text messages,
wait for a response before you send another text.
Give yourself some time to respond.
Put effort into what you are going to write in messages.
When asked out on a date, do not always say yes.
You can suggest an alternative date unless they suggest
another date first that works for you.
It is OK to send appropriate pictures, at times,
instead of saying hello with words. This can be a nice way
to spark up text conversations.

Chapter 8

Breathe

Have you ever felt butterflies in your stomach? Maybe your heart started beating rapidly, and your chest started pounding. Your palms became sweaty, or your skin started to tingle? These are all symptoms of anxiety. This is not a negative thing, as anxiety can be our friend—once we know how to control it. We need it in our lives, but it can become frustrating when it arrives on the way to our first date.

Thinking and talking about dating creates different emotions for people. Individuals who are newly single after years of commitment may experience higher levels of anxiety, compared to a person who has dated for two years and is back in the dating drill. No matter who you are, there is a spectrum of feelings you might experience on a first date, especially if you like the person you're about to meet. *This is called first-date anxiety.* The fantastic news is I'm going to help you decrease these reactions and keep you dating successfully as your anxiety dissipates.

Most of this is in your head, meaning it comes from the thoughts you think. If you think, "Oh my. I'm so nervous! How can I do this? They will never like me," well, that negative mindset will have you believing those thoughts. Let's use positive self-talk while getting ready and driving to the date. Tell yourself you look fabulous, you're ready, and if this person is not a good fit, give yourself permission to just have fun and be in the moment with another person who is searching for the same things and feelings as you.

Nervous feelings can get wrapped up with feelings of inadequacy, especially if your date is very attractive. Before you go on your date, you may need to relieve yourself and not think about sexual thoughts because sex or fooling around will not decrease your anxiety. In fact, they will super-charge it. Remember, we are searching for a *connection*, so please control your emotions and sexual appetite when dating.

You can also take five very deep breaths in the car, distract yourself (e.g., count all of the red cars you pass), or call your best friend for support. All you need to do is stop focusing on the uncomfortable feelings and get yourself excited about your date. Remember, excitement and anxiety feel very much the same.

Another way to be calm, cool, and collected is to stay in the moment and grounded. This works for anxiety anywhere. Keep your thoughts and self on that exact moment. If you are driving, think about driving, listen to your favorite songs, and relax. Each time your thoughts drift, pull them back to the moment. Anxiety is worrying about the future when nothing has happened yet. Take control and practice this skill of staying in the present moment.

Trust me, as soon as you see your date, the anxiety will start to wash away as your attention will be on them. In the meantime, remind yourself it's just a feeling, and you're going to be OK. As you date, it will get less difficult as you will have had success from prior dates to recall. In this book, I write a lot about mindset because most of dating is a mindset; it's knowing who you are and what you want. Everything else will come together.

Happy first dating. Don't forget to breathe.

Chapter 9

Be a Pretzel

Why is it that the older we get, the more difficult it is to find a relationship? Do we have more specific criteria or more expectations to meet? Could it be that we get set in our ways and are less likely to bend or loosen our routines?

Naturally, as humans, we get into habitual routines. If you are ready to meet a potential life partner, create the room, adjust, and open your mind to new things. It's a big word called *compromise*.

When dating and meeting new people, we need to be open to driving to another town or meeting at a restaurant we have never been to before. This sort of compromise is OK! You would do it for your best friend, and I'm about 100 percent sure when you were in your twenties, you did not blink an eye about these things. This is the mindset I alluded to at the beginning of this book. Your limited thought process is just in your head. Try to open your mind to more adventure rather than giving in to fear. Keep in mind that anxiety and excitement can feel the same. Try to lean toward the positive.

Location is considerably important. How close you want your potential partners to live (and how far away you'd tolerate) is a decision you will need to make when dating. I like to call this characteristic "geographically desirable." Keep in mind, too close may feel great initially, but if you break up, a little distance will undoubtedly be the best. Constantly running into ex-dates on your home turf may not be ideal. So consider focusing on a middle ground as far as distance is concerned. I like using the word *balance* because it is in the middle, and everything good is in the middle. Discovering what is too far is part of what you have to do to be more open to finding the right match. For instance, maybe for you, a one-hour drive is too far, but thirty minutes is doable. Opening up your world is way more exciting than you think!

As discussed in the chapter outlining the Ice Cream Theory, opening yourself up to new experiences and being flexible doesn't mean going against your morals and values. That is what living is all about. It is about making dating a priority and finding time and ways to adjust your routine or daily schedule for your and your date's benefit. Being rigid and unable to adapt leaves no room for a partner. Being flexible, like a pretzel, is the key.

Let's talk about what this looks like in dating. Being available means saying yes and choosing to be open to new experiences. It means being happy that you are spending time with and meeting new people. It means taking turns, exposing your likes and dislikes, and going to each other's favorite or home-base locations. It means talking when they want to or about what they want and vice versa.

Be open. New is good!

Be as flexible as a New York City hot pretzel.

Chapter 10

Rabbit Hole

No matter who you are or how strong your self-worth is, we all have disappointments when dating. It can be after the first date, a few dates in, or even at the three-month marker or beyond. These setbacks are the downside of the dating journey. It's true; it can't be all ice cream and rainbows.

We will experience those moments when we get home after a date and realize that our balloon just popped. This feeling is horrible! We may have thought they were the person we were looking for, and for whatever reason, it is now over.

When the date does not meet our expectations, it can create negative thoughts and feelings. I call this going down the **rabbit hole**. This is when all of our doubts and negative thoughts surface, and we think maybe dating is not in our cards. We may think, *I'm going to be alone forever; no one is ever interested in me; I'm never going to find my person; no one out there is for me,* or we might ask ourselves, *what is wrong with me?*

We start to be hard on ourselves and blame ourselves for the disappointment rather than looking at the positive side. We need to keep our dating journey in perspective. Dating, looking for that one person, going out, online swiping—all of this takes time. To find a healthy partner, we must stay in a slow, positive flow.

Having negative thinking is unhealthy, and it comes from our society and messages from domestication. Believing we should be with someone or married at *this point* in our lives can interfere with successful dating and the thoughts surrounding it. Yes, we want to share our lives, but there is nothing wrong with being single while looking for a healthy, happy, and vibrant partner. Stay focused on yourself and try not to let negative messages or lies jump into your thoughts and affect your mood or choices. What you really should be thinking is, "Wow dating can be complicated and time-consuming. I know I'll meet someone; it's just going to take time. I can take a break, or I can keep doing everything I'm doing."

Learning how to create a positive twist in your thinking may mean creating a new mantra. Try reciting this: *I'm amazing, enough, and attractive. My suitor is out there. I refuse to settle, and I'm worth the wait. Meanwhile, I will continue to do the things that make me happy.* It's important to practice this thinking, so you stay in a healthy mindset when dating. And remember, you just discovered this person was not for you, so now you can go out and meet your right person.

As you are dating, keep your head held high, stay positive, and redirect those negative thoughts or reframe them, to keep yourself from **falling down the rabbit hole,** as some individuals get stuck there for a while. I'm here to tell you it's not worth it, so please don't get stuck. Keep going, and you will meet your person.

Stay Positive!

Notes

Part III

Healing from your past.

Under Construction

The world is a different place than it was even fifty years ago.

When looking back to the time of our parents and grandparents, people got married and stayed married. If they divorced or became widowed, they would marry one time again or just stay on their own.

Today, in this time and era, people are marrying two, three, sometimes four times, and even if you don't marry, you may have many long-term and short-term relationships. I'm by no means saying this is a bad thing. It is our new normal, but with change, comes **evolving**. Remember when I mentioned that we only change from adverse events? Yup! After each marriage and break-up, as we say goodbye to the negativity associated with the relationship, mourning the loss of that time together, it is our chance to stop, grow, and evolve into a better version of ourselves. This prevents us from rinsing and repeating. This is the period that each of us has been missing until now.

We need to reflect on our past relationships during the mourning phase and heal, not only for ourselves but for our future relationships. We all get hurt, and that is part of our growth. We must learn what we don't want to know what we do want.

Evolving is a healing time, so I encourage you to use it before getting back into the dating scene. Find the better version of yourself!!!

Dating Tip

Set boundaries in dating!
Do not let people take advantage of you
or disrespect you.

Dating Tip

Heal yourself before
entering a new
relationship.

Chapter 11

Please Stow
Your Luggage Above

We all come into our new relationships with baggage, but it is crucial to know which bags are yours. Each of us has gone in and out of relationships in our lifetime, starting with the relationship we had with our parents. We have been hurt; we have been stuck; we have fallen in love; we have been abused, or we have stayed way too long or not long enough. We take with us all of the memories—the good, the bad, and the ugly—right into our subsequent relationships. This can be good, helping us to learn and grow into an individual who's ready for a healthy, vibrant relationship, knowing all of the bad we had to endure to get there. It can also be bad because if you don't know how to stow your luggage, it can get in the way of the relationship at hand.

Having a relationship comes with baggage and triggers. The triggers are usually what others have said or done to us in the past regarding an issue, causing us to react in the present as we did in the past through habit or a pattern we've fallen into. We don't mean to respond that way with our new partner, but it just happens. What helps is self-awareness, using our heads, and not running off of our emotions. When a partner gets you upset, the best thing to do is not react, but instead, think about why it upsets you. After you sort through the feelings and thoughts, sit down with your partner to discuss a solution or inform them that it was your trigger, and you will try to respond differently next time.

Healing from past romantic relationships and healing from childhood parental relationships are equally important. Unresolved childhood issues can continue to put you in unhealthy relationship patterns. These unresolved issues create a continual cycle, in which you might find yourself tumbling over and over again, not knowing exactly why. An example is a child who grew up in a home with addiction, abuse, or neglect, or with a mentally unstable parent. This domestication can later create certain behaviors and patterns, such as people-pleasing, insecurities, co-dependency, unhealthy boundaries, and having a high tolerance for toxic people.

Learning what your triggers are each time you end a relationship will help you in your next relationship so you do not continue to punish others for past relationship issues. Knowing your triggers—identifying them is half the battle—and changing your behavior—the other half—is important. A therapist can be very helpful in this phase. When you learn your triggers, you can handle them appropriately, not blaming but taking responsibility and coping with old emotions that will eventually dissipate in time and with trust. Ultimately, we want to keep our new dates and potential partners clear of past issues and history, as they have no bearing on where you are now. Set limits and maintain healthy boundaries.

Do not blame new relationship partners for old relationship issues.

Stow your bags so they are not flying around.

Past Triggers

T o learn to handle past triggers, you first need to *identify* the trigger. A trigger is a response to a behavior (Example: yelling). When a person yells, you shut down. Second, once you are aware of the trigger and your behavior, then you can change it. For instance, when someone is screaming, you can say, "I will speak to you about your issue as soon as you talk in a calm voice." This allows you to walk away, take a deep breath, realize you're safe, and understand your response was just your trigger. When the person is ready, you can both address the issue in calm voices.

Identify the trigger, write it down, note how you have responded in the past, and decide how you want to respond moving forward. Respond don't react.

Name the Trigger	Old Response	New Response
Yelling	Shutting down	Stating your needs directly

Chapter 12

Thank You. Next!

The first few dates you go on with a new person can be filled with many emotions: excitement, nervousness, hope, and doubt. When you are getting out there, open to meeting new people—one who may turn into a potential intimate partner—you don't want to hear about their last relationship, especially on the first few dates. I know you do not want to hear your new date talk about their ex/exes. I also know, if you are ready for a new relationship, you would not want to talk about your ex/exes. So why are people doing this? **I call it dating suicide**.

A discussion about how long you have been single or divorced and how long you have been in other relationships is acceptable. This general information is good to help navigate dating history. Still, having to listen to details about your ex (or theirs) is a turn-off.

Even after a few dates, do not share your past relationship disasters. If you were cheated on, abused, left, or did that to others, discussing it will not bode well for this new possible relationship. It is your past, and it has no place in a new, positive, healthy relationship. If you feel the desire to discuss it, therapy would be an ideal and safe place to process it, heal from it, and stow it away for good.

Past relationships are crucial to your relationship learning process to find and maintain healthy relationships. We learn what we want and don't want from a partner: better communication, compromise, and understanding other peoples' needs. Mostly, we discover how to love deeper with each new experience if we allow it.

We need to allow ourselves to learn from past relationships before we enter a new one. Having a partner and being in a relationship is *not* about not wanting to be alone. It's about sharing your life with a person who brings out the best in you and adds to your life. Having a good sense of self is ideal, which takes us back to my ice cream analogy. It is better to be alone than to be in an unhealthy, draining, and unhappy relationship.

Taking time between relationships allows you to find perspective on what you learned from that relationship and any others. Once you get through the hurt of the goodbye, which is always tricky, you should try to reflect on what kind of relationship you want moving forward. Answer these questions for yourself: What was good about the last relationship; what went wrong and how you can create a better relationship the next time around?

First, consider all of your past significant relationships.

Second, write what each person has taught you and what it was about the person you liked and did not like. For example, my ex, John Doe, led me to open my heart and not be so guarded. I liked that he was so encouraging about my career, and I want to find that again. He did have jealousy issues, which I believe to be unhealthy and in the future, is a non-negotiable red flag.

We are not perfect, and it takes two sides to make a healthy, positive, functional relationship. Oh, did I mention that relationships are hard work? If you don't want to do the work, don't be in a relationship. Once healed and ready for a stronger, more profound love—real all-in love with all your knowledge from all of your exes, whose lessons taught you to have the most amazing relationships ever—then . . . you're ready!

Below, list your past relationships, what they taught you, and the pros and cons as you assess them. This exercise should help you get an idea of what you want and don't want moving forward.

Past Relationships/What They Taught Me:

1. Name:	What They Taught Me:
Pros:	Cons:
2. Name:	What They Taught Me:
Pros:	Cons:
3. Name:	What They Taught Me:
Pros:	Cons:
4. Name	What They Taught Me:
Pros:	Cons:

Feel free to use a separate journal page so you have adequate room or simply continue this list somewhere else if you run out of space.

Chapter 13

Hot Mess

Times change fast, and the dating arenas keep morphing. It's time to learn new rules and knowledge to add to your toolbox. Now is an important time to regroup before stepping back into the dating venue. More and more people are getting out of different types of long-term relationships or marriages, with a desire to find a new partner, which creates a whole new playing field. Some people choose to end relationships and move into new ones way too soon, which creates this challenge that I call *Hot Mess*.

When you're just out of a one-year-or-longer relationship and still healing, you're emotionally unavailable. You're a Hot Mess. It's recommended not to date men or women for at least a year or more after leaving a long-term relationship because this allows you time to properly heal and learn what you need to learn before moving on. Anyone fresh out of a relationship is healing, sorting, jaded, and hurt, even though they will always tell you differently. However, if a person has been receiving professional help along the way, there is more of a chance they are healing and aware of their situation and could be more ready and open to a healthy relationship.

When wanting a relationship after a breakup, one should look for a causal relationship while healing. Nevertheless, you must be honest about it. This would be great with another person who is also recovering since you are both somewhat unsure about the future, healing from the loss of a partner or family, and you can do it together. *Two Hot Messes*! If nothing else, at least it is one way to get through that in-between period.

Unfortunately, people don't know they are a *Hot Mess,* and other people don't know either. This "unaware stage" opens the door for hurt people to hurt other people. When getting out there and looking for a partner, one needs to know what they are looking for to find the right fit. Individuals who are still healing are usually unsure of what they want. If you take dating slowly, —**taking your time and listening**—you will hear what you need to know. You will be able to identify if someone is emotionally available or not.

There is nothing wrong with taking time for you. Honestly, you have nothing to give, and in essence, what you really want is someone to make you feel better. I think that you are the best person for that job. Being single or solo for a while is amazing, and I genuinely believe it is way too underrated. Taking time for yourself, engaging in self-care, and spending time with your friends and your family are ways to keep re-defining yourself and creating a better *you*.

If you are healthy and dating, you will want tips on who is a Hot Mess.

First, find someone who has been single for a while. Maybe they have dated here and there but have not been in a serious relationship for two to three years. It is said that it takes half the time of the relationship to heal from it.

Second, listen to what this person says. They may say it all, that they are ready, they want to get married, or they never want a serious relationship again. Remember, we can't change people, so if their future does not align with yours, move on to the next!

Third, people will show their investment in you by taking you out, wanting to spend time with you, and having you meet the significant people in their lives.

Tips if you're under a year out of a break-up/divorce:

- ❏ Work on self-care
- ❏ See a therapist to process relationship
- ❏ Sleep seven to nine hours each night
- ❏ Exercise
- ❏ Eat healthily
- ❏ Take baths with salts and vitamins
- ❏ Read books
- ❏ Re-align with old and new friends
- ❏ Find new hobbies or get back into old ones
- ❏ Clean and organize your home
- ❏ Paint a room or get rid of old things that are reminders
- ❏ Journal
- ❏ Write about your healing and progress
- ❏ Set positive goals
- ❏ Make new dreams

Here are some questions to ask when dating, to learn if someone is emotionally unavailable versus emotionally available.

- Do you ever want to get married (again) or are you open to a serious commitment/engagement? (This one is a classic question. Their look will give their answer away.)

If a person has healed and they are in a good headspace, they are open. If they are unavailable, the response is close to a definitive no.

Ask any questions about the future:

- Where do you want to live or travel to or where do you see yourself in five years?

Unavailable people don't know or their answer is very self-based. People wanting to invest in someone else will see themselves with someone and have a good idea of where they want to be.

Unavailable people will always return to flirty or shallow conversation because it's safe, whereas available people want to find out more and dig deeper about you. After all, they generally want to find that right person too.

Players and narcissists will be all into you very quickly, wanting to get married, have kids, and go away to Hawaii next week. They either want to get laid and tell you what you want to hear, or they are grooming you to abuse you later. Either way, run, walk, or ghost. This is not a healthy person.

Chapter 14

Give Me Three Steps

When dating one or more potential people, you will reach a time when there is **conflict**. It can start small, such as a cancelation, running late, or a location change. Later, as dating develops, the arguments will become more significant. I call this the first disagreement or "first fight." This is a very critical moment, as you get to see exactly how this person manages and handles disagreements, how well they listen, if they're able to compromise, and how they offer solutions. It will also allow you to see their temperament, meaning their ability to regulate emotionally. This event can make or break your potential relationship.

How the other person handles conflict is extremely important, but so is how you do it. Keep in mind that you are both initially on your best behavior, and when a dispute arises, it will be the best way that person is capable of handling it. Translation: Do not think it will get easier in time. It is the exact opposite; as you both get more comfortable, handling conflict will become less effective if one (or neither) of you has the skillset, patience, and respect required.

What skills/mindset do we need to handle conflict/disagreements?

The **first step** is not to take anything too personally. It is about adjustment. If someone wants to cancel or change venues or is running late, it is OK. Just discuss a solution. A solution might be: Ask when they'd like to get together next or where they'd like to go instead, or say something like, "I'll get us a drink at the bar while I'm waiting." We are not all perfect, but in dating, the person should not get too many chances in the beginning. Only allow for a few of these events and then to set a boundary. The more they cancel and run late, the more it shows that you are not a priority—or, they may be very scattered. Either way, they may not an available suitor.

The **second step**, how they handle conflict, can reveal their ability or inability to be in a healthy relationship. If you are running late, canceled the date, or needed to change the venue, listen to their tone, hear or read their words, and carefully examine their demeanor. If they get angry, sarcastic, or won't talk to you to discuss a solution, then there is nothing left to do or say. No one should be that upset by one of these events, so pay close attention. They are showing you who they are and their inability to cope. This could be due to their past triggers or a negative attitude. Maybe they handled it like a champ, said all the correct things, and actively participated in turning the situation around. If so, that sounds like they remain a very potential candidate.

The **third step** is how you both cope with the first big disagreement. This usually arrives around the three-month marker, as the walls start to come down. It can happen earlier or later. This disagreement will be the first big one. It can be many concerns you have been holding in or one larger issue that has just occurred. Such issues can be jealousy, unhealthy boundaries, poor communication, non-transparency, lack of respect, or inappropriate behaviors. If alcohol is involved, it is not a good time to discuss any issue, but it is usually the time people feel the courage to discuss them. My suggestion is to wait until your head is clear and discuss it later . . . when substances are not altering your thinking and you can find a solution through all of your swirling emotions. When this disagreement does happen, the things you want to see from the other person are respect, the ability to listen, and resolution. Each of you must stay calm and focused on how the other person feels and ways to work through the person's concerns.

I tell my clients that disagreements, if handled correctly, only strengthen your relationship and allow you to grow closer. It can take you both to the next level of the relationship. If that does not happen, then be thankful you did not waste too much time on each other, and you can get back out there and start again. Couples can receive help to become better communicators as long as you both are on board to work on the relationship. Immediately walking away and not looking back after a disagreement would happen for the following: disrespectful name-calling, hurtful physical touch, aggressive threats, and abandonment.

This time is a great opportunity to reflect on your conflict resolution skills and make improvements on your end if you are unsure how well you handle disagreements. This is an important skill. An inability to handle disagreement in a smart manner can hinder your ability to be in a healthy, vibrant, lasting relationship. Learn how to respond to disagreements rather than react to them. How you handle conflict can mirror positive outcomes to your partner and create healthy, positive communication rather than a negative confrontation.

Be mindful of your communication and other people's conflict resolution skills. They can create an amazing beginning or a gruesome end to any dating experience.

Notes

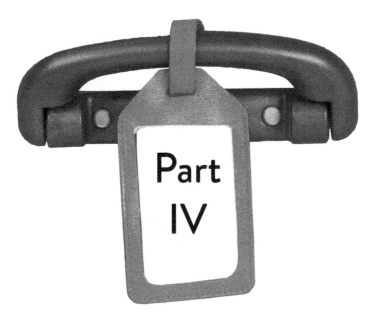

Part IV

Be mindful!

Mirror, Mirror

When creating your dating persona, you must put your best foot forward while being as grounded as possible. In other words, be your best you! When meeting someone out and about or using online dating, you need to be positive and approachable. In creating an online profile, use clear pictures of yourself taken within the last few months and a solid and brief summary of who you are and what you are looking for. This is crucial!

Let's face it; we need to sell ourselves. There are millions of single people out there, and you are one of them. Keep updating your pictures and attending events. You never know where you will meet Mr./Ms. Right!

Dating Tip

Dating is a skill to be learned,
just like playing tennis.

Dating Tip

Be positive and in a good space
when meeting people.
If you are not feeling it,
then reschedule.

Chapter 15

Collateral Damage

When looking for a long-term partner, it is important to find out information about their past trauma as soon as you can. I can tell you this from my experience and the experience of many others who found out past trauma way too late. I truly believe there are broken people out there, which does not have to be the case if people who have traumas would work through them and on themselves in therapy. Then, they would evolve.

Remember, negative events create positive outcomes if we do the work. I tell my clients all of the time that we never change and grow through positive events as we do through unfavorable circumstances. Unfortunately, some people get stuck, blame, avoid taking responsibility, and never grow from these life events. There would be way more healthy and available people out there if they did. Until this happens, we must look for what I call the "totaled vehicles." It takes around three collisions for a car to be considered totaled. Similarly, it takes three traumas for a person to be classified as *broken*.

What is considered a prior trauma? Past traumas are any type of abuse, being cheated on, alcoholism, drug addiction, accidents, divorce, death, abandonment, and other significant events that happen to a person, which change their life forever. When we meet people, we must find out about their collisions in a fun, flirty, and non-judgmental way, ideally over a series of the first three dates. At this point, you are using your brain, wearing your armor, and being fun but inquisitive. People tell you most things, but you must listen, and you must ask questions. If you miss what they say, you may not hear it again until it's too late.

Here are some questions you should ask to find out more about their past. Ask them about their *miles on their car*: "How long were your long relationships? How many relationships or divorces have you had?" Find out what kind of dents and dings are on their car from their past, which would be past break-ups, family issues, and broken friendships? How long do they hold friendships? Can they maintain friendships? Are they friendly with exes and if so, how friendly? There is a difference between seeing your ex out and saying hello and having a stay-at-home movie night with an ex. It is safe to say that being too friendly is a red flag. Also, ask about their family. Do they speak to their family? Have they accepted their family and love them for who they are? These are all parts of the big picture that will be important as the relationship develops.

Moving forward with this new knowledge, you will better navigate conversations and ask the questions you need to have answered. We all have a past, and we all have past trauma. Like ourselves, we now need to find partners who have healed and are ready to connect in healthy relationships.

Seek out healthy partners from the beginning.

Chapter 16

Where is Waldo?

Dating is an adventure, but the experience can be amazing, or it can end up being terrifying. In a world full of billions of people, you will see all kinds, and I'm here to open your eyes to the toxic, unhealthy people you want to avoid at all costs when dating.

These individuals know who they are, and they know what they want from you. They are difficult to detect, as they seem like everyone else from the outside, but they work hard to be charming and alluring. They will specifically leave out information they do not want you to know initially, due to a fear of losing you. They gravitate toward happy, sensitive, empathic humans who are stable, confident, and have it all together. They are extremely charismatic and attentive to your needs to create a connection.

A few examples to be aware of are addicts, narcissists, people with borderline personality, and psycho/sociopaths. In the chapter called "Collateral Damage," I discussed individuals who have accumulated trauma throughout their lives, who don't seek out therapy and healing. These individuals were relatively healthy until their traumas began to mount. For instance, their second wife cheated on them or their mother passed away, and she was their last parent left. (Cumulative traumas happen to people over long periods without their seeking treatment. Whereas the disorders listed above can be due to childhood abuse mixed with genetics.)

Addiction is its own animal and comes with a genetic component. It can intertwine with the other disorders mentioned above. It can also stand alone, but once an addict succumbs to drugs or alcohol, they are always an addict. Addiction changes people's lives forever. Be aware of what drugs and how much alcohol a person is consuming on the first few dates. I always ask people about their drug and alcohol history. It is good to know because if you don't ask, they probably won't tell you, and then it may be too late.

When talking about personality disorders, behaviors can range from mild to extreme. Some people display slight behaviors, so it's harder to detect. Others intentionally harm you, having honed their skills of deception to fill their own needs and emptiness. These individuals require a lot of attention, so loving, stable, empathic people fit the mold as their targets. They sweep you off your feet and "love bomb" you, which means they tell you everything you want to hear, including all of the wonderful things about your looks, your job, and just how fantastic you are. They will promise a future, family, lavish trips, and gifts. You may think you found the man/woman of your dreams after only the first few dates. It feels too good to be true! Well, then, it is! This love bombing will continue until they feel you have fallen for them, and then they slowly start to abuse you with gaslighting, word salad, manipulation, and intermittent attention. This change in behavior is how they begin to control you. Meanwhile, you have no idea what's going on. All you remember is the amazing beginning and how wonderful this person made you feel.

Here is what to look for: When on the first three to five dates, and it's starting to move fast, slow down. Stick to one to two dates per week—tops! Toxic individuals like to move quickly to throw you off your game and confuse you. It would be best to move slowly, making the toxic person go away because they will get uncomfortable and move on to someone else. Also, watch your date and the amount of their drinking throughout the date. Do they have a few drinks or are they sucking them down? Notice if they order your food or drinks without asking you what you want. Remember, asking questions throughout the date about the past and present is crucial. They won't give you the information, but if you ask them, they will reply, so listen closely. Listen to how they speak about past relationships and friend relationships; do they take responsibility for break-ups or divorces or was it everyone else's fault? Keep getting to know your date, go slowly, and keep your eyes wide open.

Healthy people don't want to fly you to Hawaii on your second date or see you every day or propose on the third date. Healthy people have a life, and they can genuinely have an interest and want to see you next week. If you have already had this experience in past dating history, try not to repeat it.

If you find you are in this pattern again or you do this to others, you may want to have a therapist help you create a new pattern, a healthier one.

You must look inside to see who people really are.

Chapter 17

Recycling

What is the definition of *goodbye*? Generally, it's defined as parting ways, which we all know means to leave. It means you have left, or they went, and the connection is now no longer.

Goodbye brings me to the word **recycle**. Why are individuals going back to a person after they have already ended the relationship? Hopefully, previous chapters have created an awareness for you regarding which people will fit in your life and which will not. You now know that you need to *be picky*, and you have learned to keep your eyes open to spot toxic and unhealthy people.

There are very few people in the world that have had success in getting back with an ex. I have also heard of a few successful marriages the second time around. I know it can happen, but more often than not, it doesn't work. I will tell you why.

First, respect yourself and your worth. Every day, I see people considering going back to old relationships after being disrespected or discarded. That means someone was hurting you verbally, physically, or emotionally. If someone loves you well, they will not intentionally hurt you. If you have been hurt, you need to say goodbye for good and find someone who will treat you with respect. Please don't think the relationship will change—just like people don't change. Relationships have patterns that we can rarely change unless we go to therapy, both willing participants in saving the relationship.

Second, learn to let go. If you were dating a person and the connection ended by them or you, then something was not working. We can't change people and make them love us, just as we cannot make chemistry or a connection that is not there. Sometimes, great chemistry and connection are there initially, and then they just fade away. This is not a good solid fit. Once again, all of this is good knowledge for you to remain aware of so you can find a strong and healthy connection that will grow.

Third, stop wasting time! Time is the most valuable thing we have besides our health. Please keep on your journey and don't look in the rearview mirror or walk backward. The time you spend breaking up and going back and forth may cause you to miss out on your right person. As I mentioned earlier in this book, the individuals who are a compatible fit need to be out there and single at the same time as you. If you are busy going back and forth with the wrong person, well, then you are not available to meet your right person. *Stop wasting valuable time!*

Use all these past relationships as learning blocks to find your match. The only thing you are missing is that comfortable attachment, and you can find that in a pet or a best friend.

Please recycle for our earth but not your love life.

Chapter 18

Table For . . .

I believe this topic is going to hit home for everyone reading this. We all need to take this topic in high regard. I spoke about who you are and what you want as far as a partner, but with a mate, may come kids. We live in an era of moderate to high divorce rates, which means meeting people who have been divorced one, two, or even three times may not be unusual. This is the new normal. You need to come to terms with whether you want a partner with kids, and if so, what ages are OK. Or perhaps you prefer a partner without kids. If so, this is something that should become part of your non-negotiables.

When dating, the hopeful outcome is finding the right person. This entails getting to know if they fit into your life and your future. In the beginning, asking the right questions and evaluating their response is vital. At first, I recommend avoiding family activities while you get to know each other as a couple. Before you go on the first date or at your first meeting is an excellent time to discuss children. Take your time and find precisely what you want in a partner.

Let's look at a few different scenarios. One is that you are single with kids (possibly due to divorce). If you have kids, one option is to want someone else with kids and then blend the two families. Both of you are aware of this situation; both of you are already raising kids and possibly involved in similar activities, and therefore, you may have a commonality in terms of family structure. If you continue to date and things progress, you might discuss blending the families after a time—say, three to six months. At the beginning of dating, you will organically decipher if you fit as a couple. You will also discover your commonalities, core beliefs, values, and how to raise your respective children, keeping in mind that focus is imperative to blending your parenting styles to further your success. Understanding and respecting each other's child-rearing styles is essential, or it may become a fork in the road. Discusses these things sooner rather than later.

The same situation but with differently aged kids or genders can create a more challenging experience than having kids the same age. Sometimes, older girls take to younger children, but it is all about your connection and ability to work together. Anything is feasible if you're invested and committed.

Perhaps your child is sixteen, and you meet someone with a three-year-old. You may not want to start over or vice versa. And that is OK! When dating, you may not want kids as part of the package at all. These are personal preferences, and there is no right or wrong answer. Knowing what's good for you and not being wishy-washy is imperative.

Some dating applications give the option of a *maybe* response regarding kids, and to be honest, dating someone for three months and then having to decide if you're interested in getting to know their kids is not fair to either of you. I have seen the heartache on both sides in this scenario, and it shouldn't be this way.

Part of being ready to date again is knowing what you want from a partner. Not knowing means you're not prepared. Most people have an idea if they want kids or a family from a young age. Some can be unsure due to their family domestication and past childhood wounds. Or some may have past issues from previous relationships that change their perspectives. Once again, I speak about healing and moving past these issues, which people do successfully every day. Make sure you're ready to share your life and decide what you want your future to look like, to the best of your ability, and then go out and find someone with a similar vision. If you want kids, you're single with kids, you're divorced with kids, or have no kids and want no kids you will meet and connect with someone. Try not to think of this as a barrier, but rather, another way for you to narrow down your best-fitting partner. Half of the equation means knowing what you want, and the other is finding it. Finding what you want is way easier than finding what you don't know you want. It will take a little longer to find it, but it is worth it.

Know the menu and who you want at your table!

Notes

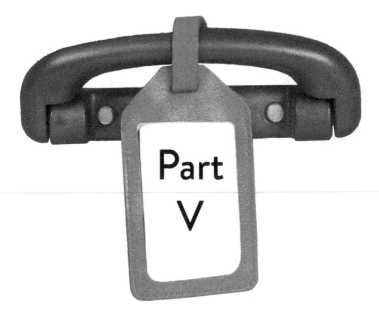

Part
V

Fill your toolbox.

Have a Kit Kat Bar

There will be days, weeks, and months when you decide that you need to take a dating break. It is time-consuming and energy-draining, to say the least. It is also fun and interesting. Besides, we are always hopeful and positive about meeting that right person. I am not the first, and I will not be the last, to tell you to take a break. When dating, we are looking for a good match, which may take a while. If you settle for just anyone, you are just wasting more time.

Sometimes, the break brings people back around that you forgot about within the dating shuffle. It can create more time to hang out with friends. Maybe revisit a few dates that you are thinking about having one more peek at. Breaktime also allows us to work on ourselves and our lives at home—maybe paint a room or write an extraordinary dating book. In other words, take some "you time." I look at it this way: whether you are seriously dating someone or are single, you are always with you. You better love "you time." **You are the most important person in your life**.

All these scenarios are a good time for reflection. Looking more closely at who you are dating, why you are dating that person, where you are meeting people, and how to change things up upon your return are all things you might consider during this time of reflection.

Stay in "break mode" until you start feeling the dating vibe again. You will know exactly what I am talking about when experiencing it. Holidays are great breaktimes and *Wheneverary*. It is healthy to take a break, as your happiness is at the top of your list, and it's a great way to keep things balanced.

Dating Tip

When using online dating,
quickly set up to meet within three to five days.
Meet-ups should be thirty to sixty minutes long;
save the rest for the first date.

Dating Tip

Know your worth,
stick to your list, and
be picky!

Chapter 19

Dogs Chase Cats . . .
But Cats Meow

Yes, dogs chase cats, cats chase cats, and dogs chase dogs. The more dominant chase the less dominant. Regardless of the type of couple you are interested in being a part of—gay, lesbian, transexual, bisexual, or heterosexual—the laws of attraction still come into play. The commonality is the role of the dominant individual and how they pursue the individual that they are interested in. This goes back to our innate instincts and our biological makeup.

Please don't take this wrong, as we can attract and have our eyes on who we want as our society is more accepting. But the more dominant partner needs to take the lead while the other person wants to be chased.

Dogs chasing cats creates more of an attraction to a masculine dater allowing the dog's interests to peak. Cats enjoy being chased by dogs. The dog's desire for the chase is in the DNA, but cats also want to feel that dogs are a challenge and are desired by other cats. It goes back to my magnet theory where at the beginning of an attraction, if one side is too aggressive or if the wrong side is aggressive, then the other person will start to become disinterested. This is because dogs are attracted to what they can't have. And if they think there is a possibility they can't have you, then you become more desirable.

Dogs are the dominant partner in the chase. Let them call, let them text, and let them come to you. Play the healthy game! Cats, there is nothing wrong with getting their attention because as we all know, dogs can be less aware of their surroundings than we cats. An attention starter, such as a first introduction, a smile, or eye contact, is the way to go. Then, it is up to the dogs to go after what they want. If they are interested, they will come to you. That, I promise! However, I must say some dogs are more introverted or shy. Those more passive dogs may meet cats in different ways, mainly in less intimidating venues. For instance, online dating or meeting through friends works better for this type of dog.

The takeaway is cats, please do not be aggressive toward dogs after the initial meet. We cannot fight primal instincts. Dogs need the chase to set up long-term feelings of attraction and attachment. On the other hand, no one wants anything to be too easy, so cats need to be less available initially, even if we like a particular dog. Dogs need to chase with an air of coyness, to keep cats interested. This means, let the cats wonder. **No one should be too available or predictable at the beginning**. A conversation will continue to ping-pong, or you will lose momentum. And please, if you're not interested, tell the individual. It is not cool to hang onto them if you don't think they're for you.

Let them chase another cat. Meow!

Chapter 20

To Sex or Not to Sex, That is the Question

This topic is somewhat controversial! Who does not like and want sex? That is what makes this chapter so intriguing and challenging, all at the same time. Most people want sex, but few have self-control when it comes to sex. When talking about dating, you must *not* have sex initially. I will tell you why . . .

First, sex is easy. Anyone can have sex, and when you like or love someone, the sex is more amazing. Sex gets better with time. There is no rush. I recommend kissing, lots and lots of kissing at the beginning. If you feel an attraction, then begin kissing on the first date.

As I mentioned earlier, sex only gets better if you wait. However, kissing does not! If the person is not a good kisser, then the odds are, they will never kiss well and are not a good match for you. Kissing is the passion within the sex, and it must be good. So kiss away.

Second, once you have sex, an emotional attraction ignites, clouding your vision and allowing you to downplay negative traits due to this attraction and desire. Suddenly, all red flags go unnoticed, and you start to rationalize the negative characteristics because the sex is so great. When letting the chemistry and desire grow, it will lead to better sex, and it will let you create an emotional attachment and an eye-opening dating experience. You will discover how much you have in common, how well you work and communicate together, and how much they respect you and your boundaries to wait. Let's get real; we kiss a lot of toads before we find our prince or princess.

Third, not having sex opens you up for sex talk, sex banter, and sex communication. The beginning is the time to discover your partner's likes and dislikes in the bedroom. With all of the communication you start to have with one another, by the time you have sex, you will know each other's likes and wants in the bedroom, making for a more comfortable and erotic first time together.

This is also a good time to get STD tests done and share the results with each other. Safe sex is essential and an excellent opportunity to discuss protection and ways to eliminate barriers in the bedroom if there is a mutual commitment.

It is essential to spend time with your date and see them around the important people and activities in your life before you introduce sex. It's called *courting*. Interestingly enough, many successful relationships started out with courting. It's the way it used to be done.

If you have sex early in the dating, you may start to rationalize the relationship as working due to the great sex, when actually, it is not clicking at all. Once you start having sex, all you want is to have sex. Sex can blind you from the important things. Once the sex balances out and you realize this person is not the best fit, it will break you up, having lost possibly a year and another six months to heal from it. All you have to do is wait on the sex at the beginning, and you will see all the incompatibilities or compatibilities. If you're not connecting, then become friends or walk away without a scratch. This will allow more wisdom in your pocket for the correct partner.

Lastly, if you are reading this book, you most likely have had one or more of these experiences: empty sex, one-night stands, sex too soon, being ghosted, the date that crashed and burned, or you keep meeting people who only want sex (casual sex or "friends with benefits"). I am thinking that now, you are open to finding an actual healthy relationship. This means, believe it or not, sex at first does not work. I suggest weekly dates for six to eight weeks before you introduce sexual intimacy. In that time, you can court each other (two months, at least.) The dates can increase in frequency at the month marker.

Sex is an important component of a successful, healthy, vibrant, and lasting relationship. When the relationship is solid, I advocate for couples to have routine sex, as it is the closest way to be with each other, and it separates an intimate relationship from a friendship.

**Be sure to keep it slow, wear your armor,
and don't have sex yet. You will thank me.** ☺

Chapter 21

Talk to Me

When speaking about communication, we are talking about how we express ourselves, our views, our feelings, and our opinions. When having a conversation, there is a give and take, an open-ended way of discovery. Each person we encounter throughout our day, whom we speak with, is an integral part of the exchange, as we use our words or our language based on that individual. Language can open many doors. I am here to teach you ways to use your words when in a dating forum.

There is verbal and nonverbal communication. Verbal communication is speaking and using words, language, and nonverbal communication is the sum of how you carry your body, your expressions, and your mannerisms. When online dating, or even meeting people out, how and what you say are your door openers. It is better to take a second to sort out the right words than to blurt out anything. It is always best to speak optimistically and enthusiastically as well.

A man walks into the bar and walks up to a woman and says how beautiful she looks and asks what she does in her free time. She replies that she enjoys all types of adventures. This may spark more playful conversation than simply saying, "Well, I don't know." At the same time that this woman is speaking with her words, if she is interested in this individual, she should have her body facing his, giving him full eye contact. Smiling is a must. Nonverbal communication says a great deal too. If you met a woman and talked to her at the bar or coffee shop and she did not make eye contact and her body did not face yours, it is a sign of disinterest.

Words are significant, and if your vocabulary is not diverse, it is best to acquire some new words. Communication is your second door opener after the initial attraction—unless you are using online dating; then, it is your first. Being playful and witty is a turn-on to most people, and you don't have to be inappropriate or too transparent to get attention. There are sexy, subtle ways of saying almost anything, which is banter at its finest. Teasing banter will be used with your partner throughout your whole relationship, and when you are apart, it will keep you connected and keep your chemistry strong.

The one thing you need first is the confidence to do any of this. You can still be shy or introverted while communicating, but having a good sense of who you are will make the process much easier. (Note: having no expectations is another must-have.) So how do you build your confidence?

Confidence is knowing that with any rejection, **it is not about you**; it is about two people who are not connecting. It may be about timing, chemistry, or non-commonalities! We all need to accept that not everyone is going to find us attractive, and we are not going to be attracted to everyone either. Guess what? It is OK!

Let us touch on expectations since we mentioned them above. Don't have them! I cannot emphasize enough what a relationship killer coming in with expectations can be. Can you read minds? Then you cannot expect someone to do anything unless you ask them. Avoid expectations, and if you already have some, let them go.

Another vital skill that comes with communication and conversation is listening. We are talking to this person because we have an interest, and we want to find out more about them. We use conversation to ask questions—usually open-ended ones to get information. Half of this skill is using active listening to hear what people are saying and to pave the way so you can ask more questions about their answers.

You meet your date for coffee, and he or she asks about your interests. You respond. Then, what if they start speaking about their interests, never responding to yours? The odds don't look very good for them. Being genuinely interested in someone means you want to hear about what makes them tick, their interests, their dreams, and their thoughts. If someone is actively listening, they are actively interested in you.

What are things you can talk about in conversations when meeting new people? After the initial greeting of *hello, how is your day,* delve deeper into who they are. It is necessary to identify a person's depth to see if you can connect authentically. Remember, people love to talk about themselves, and it is always a safe bet, but make sure there is give and take.

Ask anything, but remember to have fun and keep it positive.

Chapter 22

Balance

Balance is defined as an even distribution on both sides.

We all have times when we lean more to one side in certain areas of our lives. Perhaps, we experience a sort of imbalance at work, with exercising, in the way we spend money, or by eating too much or too little. The secret to life is **balance** everywhere and all the time. Maintaining balance is generally not easy, but a healthy skill to have.

In this chapter, I will talk about balance in a dating forum. I will explain why balance is important and what happens when you get off-balance at the beginning stages of a relationship. As far as staying balanced and not going too fast or too slow, please refer to the Ice Cream Theory. I intend to help you decipher when to **stay in** and when to **walk away** at the beginning of a relationship.

Knowing your commitment level is best demonstrated early in the relationship as you and your new person get to know each other and start growing through your differences together. (This could be when you are still dating a few people at once, or it can be after you decide that you want to focus solely on one person.) You must evaluate if you both can adjust and cope with each other, accept each other's imperfections, understand triggers from the past, and tolerate each other's quirks. It takes time to get to know your new interest, and it is wise to get them into different venues to do so. These include out socially with friends, around family, around co-workers, maybe even away on a short vacation somewhere close. You are learning about this person to see if you're both compatible or flexible with each other's needs.

This book, at times, may seem repetitive due to overlapping information that will reinforce these healthy skills. You must recognize that when certain red flags or concerns pop up as time goes on, and you both become more comfortable with each other, you first need to file the red flag away to review later if it should happen again. Another thing you will need to decide is if it continues, will it become a bigger problem later down the road. Let us take jealousy for example. In a relationship, jealousy can be healthy at a low level. For instance, saying to your date, "You looked so hot last night. It kind of made me jealous when everyone looked at you, but I know you were my date, so it was sexy" works. This is healthy jealousy. However, after leaving a party with your date, they argue with you that you were not by their side enough, telling you that you made them feel left out when you spoke to other people. If you were doing nothing out of character from past parties with this person, this is unhealthy jealousy. Dating someone who is insecure and jealous only gets worse.

Let's talk about past wounds and events that are still an issue early in the dating relationship. As I discussed in "Stowing Your Luggage," find out if your potential partner has stowed their luggage or determine if their triggers are too intense for you. They may know what their triggers are and not handle them as they arise. If it interferes with the relationship, it can be the beginning of a more significant issue. Also, therapy may be helpful if they did not work on their past and it's still upsetting them, as this can create arguments. The number one reason couples have issues later in relationships and marriages is that they never worked on childhood or past relationship issues. *Please, stow your luggage.*

Also, ask yourself if you can live with this person's habits, quirks, and imperfections. We all have them. Maybe they smoke or have daily rituals they enjoy, or perhaps they bite their fingernails or talk to everyone wherever you go. The question is, do these behaviors annoy you, or are they cute and endearing? Remember, **we can't change people,** and these tiny irritations can ultimately get magnified, creating a negative, unsalvageable issue.

If we were to look at a globe of the world, knowing there are billions of people living and single, I believe there is an average of one hundred people out there who fit you and your compatibility. Take a deep breath and don't worry. They are out there; it is just a question of meeting them. Meeting someone won't happen sitting on your couch unless your laptop is on your lap open to a dating site.

I like to refer to meeting your compatible people as timing and having found your balance. When you're healthy and have stability, you attract other healthy people who have balance. In turn, you create more possibilities for meeting and finding the person with the connection you desire. If you're dating someone you are sure is not for you, but you continue to date them, you prevent yourself from meeting the right person. You don't want to stay with Mr. or Ms. Wrong while you could be meeting Mr. or Ms. Right!

Let's face it, what are the odds of you being open and available at the same time one of your compatible partners is? EXACTLY!

That is why we don't want dating to be more complex than it needs to be.

Find your balance!

Chapter 23

007 Me!

One of the most dangerous and coolest items ever invented was the cellular phone. Not only can you get in touch with anyone at any time, but you have the world of knowledge at your fingertips. In the dating world, a cell phone can create a plethora of problems, or it can make you a dating mastermind. You can find a date, plan a date, and confirm a reservation on your phone. I want to give you strategies to help you navigate texting pitfalls, to get you on the top of your game.

One mistake everyone makes when texting is they forget that someone is going to get this message on the other end. Some people equate this to using a credit card, that the money and the text messages go into this black hole, and it just doesn't matter. I am here to tell you otherwise! Yes, you need to pay back the money, and yes, the recipient of the text message will read it and have feelings about what you wrote . . . and it may not necessarily be the reaction you intended to receive. Text and spend wisely!

When sending text messages, be certain the significance of what you are trying to communicate is clear and thoughtful. I am involved in daily message translation between clients and friends. I often feel I need a decoder ring to decipher some messages. Sometimes, we need to pick up the phone and call people to have proper communication and to create less room for assumptions, miscommunications, and drama, especially if we are upset. Texting is not the best option to discuss feelings or important material. Set a date and time to talk.

Then, there is what I call "text bombing," which is an angry blow-up of one's assumptions, and by the time the person reads those texts, the situation has gotten out of control. There is just no coming back from it. It is as hard to unsee a bad scene as it is to unread a nasty text. This relates back to my chapter "Wear Your Armor," but with regard to a text scenario instead. It is better to remain silent than to rant in a text message. It's not attractive or respectful, and the outcome will always be negative. Space and silence are your best bet until you can come together and discuss the issues or concerns.

Text messages were invented as a bridge between a pager and landline and were meant as a method of leaving a message for a person. For example, *I'll call you after the meeting; I'm running late,* or *I'll see you at 6 p.m.* The text message is not the platform to write a dissertation about your feelings. Important issues, like feelings for one another, should be addressed one-on-one or in a voice communication. Save your thoughts for when you can have a real back-and-forth, explicit talk. The best communication is done face-to-face to identify facial expressions, truly hear their voice, and feel their emotions. There is a text option to use the voice recorder to record your voice and send it directly to the person to hear as a text option. Once again, voice recording should be used with an understanding that it is a voice recording, a better option for a funny story or to get out information to another person. This way, the person can hear your voice, tone, and emotions. Voice recordings create less room for misinterpretation.

Newer generations are not learning the correct social cues and how to handle face-to-face conflict, which is a learned skill to resolve a disagreement. They use texts for all interactions, not practicing their in-person social skills, which they will need later in life. Unfortunately, people hide or rely on text messages to better cope with or avoid negative confrontation.

What about emojis? How many people even know what they mean? Emojis can be a fun way to bring emotion into texting. Well, I'm not sure they help promote better communication, but they sure are adorable.

Let's turn it around. We can't change people, but we can change our interactions. We can start having more conversations in-person versus texting, and we can stop using or relying on the text message when having something to say that needs an in-person response.

Let's address positive, appropriate uses of text messaging, which is an amazing technology when used correctly.

First, text when you need to tell someone a quick message: *I'll be there in five minutes; I'll call you later; I must work late,* or *let's have dinner at 7 at your favorite place.*

Second, use text messages to send dates cute, sexy, healthy game messages, such as a picture, *I can't wait to see you later, I had such a great time last night, I'm still thinking about our date,* or *I really adore that smile.*

Third, use texting to check-in: *Hope you're having a great day! Can I see you later? Want to grab a drink after work? How are you feeling today?*

These are appropriate ways to use text messaging.

Be prepared for the unexpected when licensed to text.

Notes

_____

_____

_____

_____

_____

_____

_____

_____

_____

_____

_____

_____

_____

_____

_____

_____

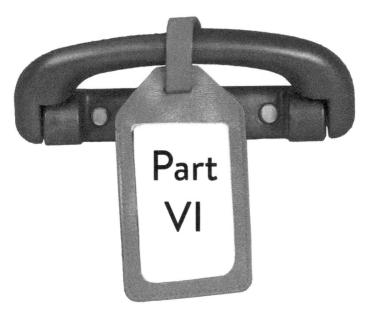

Part
VI

Extra, Extra!

The Oxygen Theory

aking care of YOU comes first! Some people would say this is selfish! That is not the case. If you're not healthy and you're not at your best, how on earth will you take care of others? Eventually, you will be tired, sick, or emotionally drained, just giving people your bare minimum.

Continually living and dating with unresolved issues is when you need the *Oxygen Theory*. You know it. You are on an airplane and the attendant reads off the safety rules: When in need of OXYGEN, pull down the face masks from above and place the oxygen mask on yourself FIRST, then on your child/ren or the elderly. Whether flying in an airplane or through life, you can't help anyone if you are depleted, pass out, or die.

Please take care of yourself first!

Filler Dating

When a relationship ends, no matter who ended it or why, it's never an amazing feeling. Breakups provide time to process where you are in life and what you want in the future. It's a great time to recapture what you learned from each of your partners, bringing growth to your life. Also, it is when you should refocus on yourself and create the changes you want to see in yourself. Spend time with friends and family.

I'm a big advocate of getting back out there and engaging in *filler dating* or, what some call, *casual dating*. This means that you are getting to know new people, keeping your feet wet, and being honest about where you are with your availability. We know you're not ready to get serious, but it is a great time to start making more friends and continue to heal from your last relationship.

A filler date is a casual date informing the other person you are newly out of a relationship and seeking a night of *companionship.* This allows you both the benefit of the company without any expectations or false hope. Since this is a very short-term situation, I will let you make your own decisions about what you do during that date. You really can't mess up a short-term, numbing experience while you heal. But you can hurt an available date, so please make sure they understand that you are not available for a relationship at this time.

Dating Tip

Be flexible when dating.
Respect each other's time.

Dating Tip

Use the ice cream cone analogy
to discover and affirm
you and your worth.
Then use it as a guide to learn
about your date initially.
Connecting on the inside first
is the key after the initial attraction.

Chapter 24

Reputation

Why does online dating have such a bad reputation?

With all of the growth and technology in the world, I would think it would be a natural transition to want to date online. I mean, really! One day we are going to be able to buy a robot partner on Amazon. Ha!

In the meantime, online dating is just another venue to meet a partner, and you may find it is more practical and more adaptable than you ever thought it would be.

Who does not like to shop for something they want? With online dating, you are shopping for a partner from your couch—or possibly while hanging out with friends. Their profile gives you a description of their general characteristics and what they are looking for in a partner. If they are emotionally available and want to invest in a partner, they will create a paragraph about themselves, who they are, and what they desire.

We are busy individuals with careers, children, hobbies, families, and perhaps a pet. Taking the time to go out and attend parties or events each week can be a bit challenging given our schedules. Online dating allows us to meet people at our convenience. We make connections with people when we have time. And we can speak to them to see if they have commonalities when we have breaks throughout the day.

During those times, ask questions, referring to the non-negotiables you have, and get into other significant inquiries so you don't waste your time pursuing something that isn't going to materialize. I'll get more into these questions in this chapter.

Then, if you continue to have an interest in one another, set up a "meet and greet" for about thirty minutes for your first outing to evaluate if there is chemistry and if they are **"date-worthy."** Please keep it to thirty minutes maximum because you will both know in that time frame if there is enough interest to move forward. Either way, leave after thirty minutes. Going after this short stint, no matter how much you like the other person, keeps you desirable, allowing the official first date to be set up.. If you or they did not find interest, get back online.

I will keep telling you how valuable your time is, and this is another important reminder to keep your time in check. It is easy to carve out thirty minutes for coffee or a cocktail and get right back to your life. Your first date will be a whole evening out, which is an evening where you are free to do whatever you want. This day or night may entail babysitters or pet sitting or missing the weekly friend slot. Make sure you like this potential person, and they are worthy of your time before you agree to go.

Bada Bing, Bada Bang! Just like that, you can be going on dates and do not have to throw yourself into a crowded bar or go to the neighbor's party down the street—the one that always makes you uncomfortable.

I genuinely believe you should attend and be part of everything when you are ready to share your life. You can meet people anywhere. I hear stories of how people meet online and out and about. People meet at grocery stores, gatherings, parking lots, crossing the street, parties, and coffee shops. It's about being open and available; it can happen just about anywhere (timing and readiness). I now have many clients and friends in serious relationships from online dating.

Let's get back to those initial online questions. Ask your date how long they have been single or divorced. Ask about health and wellness. Ask about kids and how many they have or how many they want or don't want. At this point, you are just getting some information to lead up to the meet and greet, but please keep it light and fun. If you ask questions, it can come off as a job interview and create a turn-off. So get in a few and then stop. Be fun and witty. Also, never forget to get a selfie of both of you before you arrive. There is nothing like showing up and having them look nothing like their picture. What a waste of time! UGH!

Tips for online dating:

When talking to someone, set a meet and greet within the first three to five days of texting. If you are comfortable, give them your phone number and have them send a selfie, and if it is not consistent with the online picture, block the number. Your cell number is public information. If the picture matches, then meet with them.

Get their last name before the meet and greet. Google them to make sure nothing unsafe comes up. Always let someone else know where you are meeting. People often forget to do this, and it is extremely important.

Make sure your profile is current and complete. The more you write in your short, clear paragraph, the more it will assist potential suitors in knowing what you want and if you both share the same interests. Remember, available people fill their profiles out, while unavailable people don't because they don't know what they are looking for.

My Dating Resources

Free online dating services in my area:

_____

_____

_____

_____

_____

Paid online dating services in my area:

_____

_____

_____

_____

_____

Chapter 25

The Essentials

will share with you the markers I've learned along the way. They are not steadfast rules, just essentials to dating to keep in mind when going through the process at different stages. Some of you may know and have simply forgotten these things, and for others, they may be new to you. Either way, these are all informative markers to keep in mind throughout the dating process.

The three-day call: when a man meets a woman out, or after going on the first meet and greet, he will generally wait three days to call. This way, he doesn't look too eager. Please don't panic if you don't receive a call or text before then. No one wants to be too available.

When using online dating sites, after you connect with a person and begin talking with them, you generally have three to five days to pull the trigger and ask to meet them out. It will fizzle out if you wait too long, as other people will start to get into the mix. Don't miss your opportunity.

There is no three-date sex marker. A player invented that to get action, and if they don't have sex, they walk. Either way, you should wait. It is way too soon.

The three-month marker is when the walls start coming down, and the person's true colors start to become exposed. This point allows you to see the real individual, with their quirks and habits.

The first disagreement or fight generally happens around three to six months into dating, give or take.

The six-month marker is another milestone in the relationship where the walls continue to come down, and you may view the relationship as something that will be stable and lasting while continuing to work through your differences to create a deeper connection.

The final marker is the one-year marker. You look at your partner at this stage, and you can see them in your future, not wanting to continue the journey without them. If you can't see them or the conflicts outweigh the positives, it may be time to end the relationship.

Chapter 26

Catch Up!

What are the current phrases and lingo in the dating world today? Dating lingo may be something you want to know. It's a playful language when communicating with friends. As I always say, information is power and adds a layer to your character.

When using dating applications on your phone or computers sites that use the swipe method, know that if you're interested, you swipe to the right, and if you're not interested, you swipe to the left. In conversations with groups of people, you may hear someone say swipe to the right to inform the group that a good-looking person just walked by.

Online dating terminology is for all age groups, like the expression *Netflix and chill*. I would hope you would know at any age what this means, but I know high schoolers use it. You are not actually watching Netflix, but it is on.

On the other hand, more adults use the term *ghosting* in their dating lives. People don't like confrontation, and ghosting provides a simple out. Ghosting is when you suddenly disappear from someone's life after you have been spending time with them. Later, you may use the term *haunting* if they return by contacting you in some social media forum.

I mentioned earlier that simultaneously dating a few people is a great way to go if you can manage it. When dating different people, you may "bench" the other dates to determine who stays and who goes as you find better candidates. When you find someone you like, you should DTR (define the relationship).

We all have a new awareness and understanding of hand sanitizer these days, so naturally, the term *sanitizing* caught my eye. After you break up with someone, delete them or wipe them clean from your social media. They no longer exist; they have been sanitized.

I tell you to date multiple individuals initially but to remain open and honest about it. Lying about it or attempting to hide it, is called *roaching*. Yuck!

Have you ever had someone reach out to you on dating sites or social media, but they never have a picture of what they look like anywhere? Not only is that a red flag but it is also called *waldo-ing*.

Also, when dating multiple individuals, you may *breadcrumb*, which means you are leading your date on only for attention, not because you are interested in a relationship with them. If you're dating someone very attractive but who is boring and has nothing to bring to the table, this is called *white clawing* (iHeart Radio).

iHeart Radio mentioned that when a person asks for your number and you give it to them, but when they call or text and you don't respond, you're not responding is called *dial toning*.

Ever get all dressed up and been super excited to go out on a first date, and then, suddenly, they cancel? That's called being *glamboozled.*

Isn't this fun?

There are many more terms, and new ones are continually being generated. Google "dating lingo" and have a few laughs. These terms can be great openers to strike up a conversation on a first date. You can even use them in your texting banter.

Have fun!

Chapter 27

Dating Disasters
(There is never a dull moment
in dating. Enjoy the ride!)

Here are some people's stories about first, second, or third dates before finding their right person. Some dates will be bad, some funny, and some will validate your incompatibility, while others may take more time. Let's learn to laugh it off. Each story below has been kept anonymous and close to their words.

"On one of my first dates, my date told me to look no more, he was the perfect man for me. With a straight face and a serious voice, he proceeded to discuss his current substance abuse and abandonment issues at the restaurant table. I went to the bathroom and never returned."

"I showed up to the date, and it was not the same person as the picture—from twenty years ago."

I have heard this dating story about thousand times. People lie or just leave out the information about their age, height, hair, lack of hair, weight, or anything people feel insecure about. Get people to send pictures or video chat before a date.

"On a second date, after a nice romantic dinner, we entered an Irish pub, and I put my hand in something wet on the table. The bar was filled, and I proceeded to ask the gentlemen sitting there to pass me a napkin. When he passed me the napkin, my date proceeded to yell at me about how little respect I had for him to pick up a dude at the bar right in front of him. At first, I laughed, thinking he had to be kidding, but no, he was serious and mad. I told him I'd find a ride home and thanked him for dinner and left."

"After being single for one year after my break-up, I was set up on a blind date by a new friend of mine, and when I arrived, it was my ex. How awkward was that?"

"After having a nice drink and appetizer while looking at the ocean, we proceeded to the hotel pool to drip our toes in. After I used the restroom, he asked if I would like to go to the champagne room. I said sure. Little did I know he meant champagne in a hotel room. Umm."

"I picked up a girl from a hotel who I met online. We went to lunch. She later told me she was homeless."

"On our first date, after talking daily for a week, he picked me up and drove me to the restaurant swerving all over the road. At the restaurant, his behaviors were arrogant and cocky. I left as soon as I had the chance, having a guy friend spend the night for security. The date showed up at 6 a.m. looking for all his belongings, saying he was robbed and didn't remember anything from the night before except our meeting."

"After our first date, I walked her out to her car at 10 p.m., and at 4 a.m., she called me to get her from the police station because she had gotten a DUI."

"On our third coffee date, we made out in the parking lot, and his mouth tasted so bad that after one more date, I just could not go on. I doubted there was a solution. The guy was the package too."

"Before our first date, I spoke to him on the phone to gauge his personality and start assessing him for flags. He said he had seven kids, a Pitbull service dog for PTSD, could only date during the week, and would have to go a day before our date to where we would be meeting to 'feel it out.' I chose not to meet him after all."

"On our first date, he told me all of his problems, which were a lot—the death of his parents and a career change. Then, he told me how rich and successful he was while adding, by the way, 'I currently downsized to a trailer home.' All these inconsistencies made him undesirable to me."

"On our first date/meet-up, he wanted me to meet him and his friends at a local bar. I said sure. After hanging for a while, his roommate became catatonic at the bar. No one could wake her. They called 911. I thought, 'This is your best friend! What kind of drugs are you guys taking?'"

"On our first date, she asked if she could stay over in a very sweet flirtatious way. It was not my way, as I like to wait. She finally told me she needed a ride to the Methadone clinic in the morning, and it was close to my house."

"On our first date, he did not say one word during dinner; he just looked at me."

I hear about the boring dates, the quiet dates, and the uncomfortable ones. If you feel there is something—an attraction, a commonality, or a good vibe—go out again if you have the opportunity. It may be nerves, anxiety, and uncomfortableness on that first date. Sometimes, people warm up and surprise you.

"I went to pick up my date, and my car broke down in the middle of the street, and we had to push the car to the restaurant."

"I was on a first date, and she brought her trained service dog with her. She said she had narcolepsy and the dog barks to wake her up. First, she shared food with the dog, using the same fork, and then she went to the bathroom asking me to hold her dog, later calling me to bring the dog to her because she was fearful she would fall asleep in the bathroom. Needless to say, I cut the date short."

"On our first date, we went and sat at an outdoor restaurant. We had spoken on the phone a few times, and we both felt comfortable. We were really enjoying ourselves. He went to the bathroom, and it took a long time, twenty-five minutes or so. I'm thinking, 'This guy is taking a deuce on our date. Gross!' He came out shortly after explaining how he was stuck in the bathroom. He was hoping I would send someone in. It was pretty funny."

"I went on a second date with a man who, when I got up to go to the bathroom, proceeded to go to the bar and have five shots, thinking I wouldn't see him do it. I did and left shortly after."

"I took this super attractive woman to this outdoor bar in the fall. I had a fuzzy zippered sweatshirt on, and there were real candles on all of the tables. I leaned over to kiss her, and my sweatshirt caught on fire. She left by the time I put the fire out."

"On our second date, I took this doctor on the boat, and we were having a great time, but I did not feel she was into me. She slipped on the boat and fell. I leaned down to kiss her, and she slapped me. I never saw her again."

"On our first date, she asked me to be her sperm donor. I asked if she meant do I want kids? She responded, 'No, just to be the sperm donor.' I wasn't interested and that was our last date."

Chapter 28

Let's Wrap It Up
(A Summary/Conclusion)

I hope you all found a helpful piece of information or the self-awareness you were looking for while reading this book and are now more equipped to discover what you want in a partner. You are ready to start your search! I wish I could give you a more detailed step-by-step approach. Each individual and relationship dynamic is so unique that it becomes personalized, requiring individualized therapy to assist in your dating journey.

In your journey, you must be healed and aware of triggers that past relationships have created. Then, you are ready to meet your partner with an open heart for new love. By this time, you have found your self-worth and have seen how truly amazing and deserving you are of finding an equivalent suitor. Dating is genuinely a wonderful but challenging process, and we cannot miss any part of it.

Your journey will not be easy, and there will be days when you want to give up. Remind yourself that greatness does not come without effort. Take your time, do the work, use the skills, and find your person. I hope I gave you a plethora of information to think about and digest and encouraged you to think in new ways. This book is always here for you to go back to review. Think of it as a reference book.

I trust these chapters have helped you build an air of confidence and provided you with hope as you ready yourself to get out there and live your best life. Keep searching for the right person to share it with you. Finding a suitable someone is not a race, so enjoy the journey.

It takes confidence and acceptance to be on your own for a while when in search of your partner. This is healthy and exciting. Enjoy creating your ice cream cone and take your time choosing whom to spend your life with while recognizing your non-negotiables and any red flags. Take pride in your life and hobbies, and be a little selfish. As you meet potential suitors, wear your armor, play healthy games, and do your part in the chase.

Take your time meeting someone authentically, spiritually, and intellectually desirable. Break out of your comfort zones and engage in new interests, knowing your boundaries, as they will be tried. Learn your triggers and practice coping with them. Be thankful your exes taught you what you don't want, and maybe what you do want, and use that as a guide. Handle conflicts with poise. Learn about and be aware of the people who are not on the same page, who are unavailable, or who are just not capable of holding your amazing heart.

Finally, do not go back. When it's over, it's over. Brush off the past and keep moving, even if it is slowly. You are not alone; you are your best company. There is a big world out there, and your partner is waiting.

**Enjoy the ride. You now have all the tools
and knowledge to get what you truly want.**

Chapter 28

Your Dating Checklist

Below is a checklist for your completed tasks and newfound knowledge. Be aware of the items in need of work or attention.

❐ I have a good sense of self-worth and identity.

❐ I am ready to identify what I want from a partner.

❐ I know what my non-negotiables are.

❐ I have a good understanding of who I am.

❐ I can adjust to new situations and people.

❐ I have healthy boundaries and can set them with others.

❐ I have patience, as I know it will take time to find a good healthy partner.

❐ I am healed from my past relationships, and I'm ready to find a new, healthy partner.

❐ I have healed from my childhood wounds.

❐ I feel confident about assessing my dates for red flags and commonalities.

❐ I will keep my emotions in check when dating.

❐ I will play only healthy games while dating and feel comfortable doing so.

❐ I will prepare for first dates to lessen first-date anxiety.

❐ I will prioritize self-care, as self-care is of utmost importance.

❐ I am aware of my past triggers; I take responsibility for them, and I'm working on coping with them in my life.

❐ I am aware of the pros and cons of my past relationships, have healed from them, and am utilizing these lessons as needed for future relationships.

❐ I acknowledge the need to have healthy boundaries, and my partner does as well.

❐ I want someone who can handle conflict. I have become much better at handling conflict too.

❐ I am aware if I want or do not want children of my own and am either prepared (or do not desire) to raise other people's kids.

❐ I must be mindful of others' past and mental health because people don't change unless they want to.

❐ I realize when a relationship is over, I must let go and move forward.

❐ I think dating breaks are a good idea from time to time.

❐ I let dogs chase and let cats get their attention.

❐ I will abstain from sexual activity at the beginning of dating to get to know them and see if they fit in my life.

❐ I am vigilant about my verbal and non-verbal communication and text messaging.

❐ I always try to stay balanced.

❐ I date using every opportunity and technology.

❐ I use ping-pong to keep things smooth in conversations.

❐ I learned new trendy dating lingo to stay current in our times.

❐ I know I am not alone and that feeling alone is not a reason to date.

❐ I will continue with self-growth throughout my lifetime.

❐ I'm enjoying my dating journey.

# Completed	# to Work On

Chapter 30

How to Get Out There and Start Dating

Internet Dating

Look up internet dating in your area (Google "best sites in your area") and get on some paid or free dating sites. You can quickly find possible dates using a swipe method, or you can sign up for paid ones that run you through some basic assessments first. You can date based on preferred age, sexual preference, religion, and so on. In the first chapter, we narrowed down what you want, so that should make this process easier.

Matchmakers

There are many levels of matchmakers—individuals or companies that look for your match if you need help or don't have the time. Some can cost $50,000, and others might be a couple hundred dollars. This service considers exactly what you're looking for and how large an area you want to include in your search.

Singles' Events

You can find meet-up groups and singles' events through the internet, your church or temple, in the paper, or at local community centers. Get their monthly calendars to plan out interesting events and put them in your calendar.

Friend and Neighborhood Parties

Just keep saying yes! Go to as many parties, gatherings, get-togethers, or hangouts as you can. You never know who will show up. It could be a new friend that will introduce you to new friends that can open a door. We need to stay involved and in attendance.

Social Media

The internet is an amazing social platform. You can meet people on any social site: Facebook, Instagram, or Snapchat. Some people even use Offer Up and other selling/buying applications to ask people out.

You've got this!

Notes

_____

_____

_____

_____

_____

_____

_____

_____

_____

_____

_____

_____

_____

_____

_____

_____

_____

_____

About the Author

Marlisse Testa, L.M.H.C, Q.S. has been a psychotherapist in Boca Raton, Florida for over twenty years. She is currently working in private practice at Testa Counseling, LLC. She is trauma-trained, a certified Nutritional and Integrative Medicine mental health professional, and a qualified clinical supervisor. Marlisse works as a general therapist but particularly enjoys helping individuals heal from their past to find the healthy, happy love they deserve. In *Stow Your Luggage When Dating*, Marlisse divulges a unique skillset for successful dating, the same tools she imparts to her clients. Marlisse has created this book to help create awareness and understanding of some of the roadblocks that prevent people from having lasting healthy relationships.

Marlisse is available for one-on-one personal counseling both in-person and virtually to provide you with a more individualized step-by-step approach.

A free ebook edition is available with the purchase of this book.

To claim your free ebook edition:

1. Visit MorganJamesBOGO.com
2. Sign your name CLEARLY in the space
3. Complete the form and submit a photo of the entire copyright page
4. You or your friend can download the ebook to your preferred device

A **FREE** ebook edition is available for you or a friend with the purchase of this print book.

CLEARLY SIGN YOUR NAME ABOVE

Instructions to claim your free ebook edition:
1. Visit MorganJamesBOGO.com
2. Sign your name CLEARLY in the space above
3. Complete the form and submit a photo of this entire page
4. You or your friend can download the ebook to your preferred device

Print & Digital Together Forever.

Snap a photo

Free ebook

Read anywhere

CPSIA information can be obtained
at www.ICGtesting.com
Printed in the USA
JSHW051930141022
31699JS00001B/7